ALL ABOUT ANGELS

THE SONG OF MICHAEL

FREDDY HAYLER

What People Are Saying about the Song of Angels series

"Have you ever gazed out the window of an airplane into a sea of clouds, or lay on your back in the grass on a lazy summer afternoon watching the clouds float by? If there were music in those clouds, how would it sound? Freddy Hayler offers us a taste of that aerial symphony. Brilliantly combining majestic melodies that stir the soul with lyrics that stir the spirit, *Song of Angels* takes the listener on a journey to the heavenlies. Relax, picture that lazy summer afternoon, and listen to and read the *Song of Angels*."

—Bob Weiner, Evangelist
Youth Now Ministries

"I love to listen to his music and hear his message and be there when he worships in his own inimitable style."

—Tommy Tenney
Evangelist
Author of *The God Chasers*

"A fresh, new sound of heaven with a powerful, prophetic message best describes this new project entitled *Song of Angels*. True worship was never intended to be an entertainment media, but was intended to be an outward expression of a deep, inward love for our creator God. Freddy Hayler's album and book are on the cutting edge of the era leading us back to true worship and holiness. Experience God's presence through this refreshing, new sound of God's prophetic voice in this new hour of 'Golden Alter' worship."

—Dick Reuben, Evangelist
Sound of the Shofar Ministries
Teacher and leader, Brownsville Revival

"Are we sincerely hungry for a genuine visitation from God? Are we truly willing to pursue the Lord regardless of the cost? The music and message of Freddy Hayler help to issue a clarion call for this nation...to cry out to God in heartfelt repentance."

—Stephen L. Hill, Evangelist
Awake America Ministries

ALL ABOUT ANGELS: THE SONG OF MICHAEL
WITH CD INSERT

ISBN-13: 978-0-88368-494-8
ISBN-10: 0-88368-494-2
Printed in the United States of America
© 2006 by Freddy Hayler

Whitaker House
1030 Hunt Valley Circle
New Kensington, PA 15068
www.whitakerhouse.com

Library of Congress Cataloging-in-Publication Data

Hayler, Freddy, 1955–
   All about angels : the song of Michael / Freddy Hayler.
         p.   cm.
Summary: "Discusses angels: who they are, what they are like, what their purpose is, and the reformation the church needs to experience angelic ministry"—Provided by publisher.
   ISBN-13: 978-0-88368-494-8 (hardcover with cd insert : alk. paper)
ISBN-10: 0-88368-494-2 (hardcover with cd insert : alk. paper) 1. Angels—Christianity. I. Title.
                  BT966.3.H39 2006
      235'.3–dc22   2006029068

1 2 3 4 5 6 7 8 9 10   **W**   12 11 10 09 08 07 06

Contents

Dedication

All praise, glory, and honor to the "King of angels"—the Lord Jesus Christ! I am extremely grateful to Whitaker House Publishers in New Kensington, Pennsylvania, for their willingness to publish and distribute this vital message to God's people around the world.

Angels are the dispensers and administrators of the divine beneficence toward us; they regard our safety, undertake our defense, direct our ways, and exercise a constant solicitude that no evil befall us.

—John Calvin

Preface: Divine Expectation

All About Angels is a prophetic word given to the church that will both warn and help prepare her for the coming reformation and holiness revival movement that God is raising up on the earth in this hour. It's my prayer that the message, music, and lyrics will stir your heart in a fresh way to seek the face of God. It is God's desire that His bride become prepared in the beauty of holiness, ready to meet her Bridegroom upon His soon return.

In this addition to the Song of Angels series, I have also included a more in-depth look at angels—their nature and especially their operations as they relate to the bride of Christ. (See Ephesians 5:25–27.) After all, isn't that what the ministry of angels is all about?

> *Are they not all ministering spirits, sent forth to minister for them who shall be heirs of salvation?* (Hebrews 1:14)

Primitive Roots

We need to return to the firm spiritual moorings of the early church. This is true not only in the area of pure doctrine and holy living but it is also true in regards to returning to the supernatural roots in which the church was founded and birthed. (See Acts 1–12.) Hyper-dispensationalists and cessationists aside, the early church had a correct perspective of angels and even expected them to show up at their prayer meetings!

Thus, the question today is, do we have the same *expectation* that the early church had regarding the ministry of angels? Do we truly believe or expect angels to show up in glorious fashion and assist us in proclaiming the gospel? Do you truly believe in angels?

Divine Expectation

The kingdom of God operates by the law of faith. If someone has no faith or has no expectation to believe in angels then it's highly unlikely that they will be open to receiving their ministry. However, unlike

ANGELIC MINISTRY

New Age religion, Christians should not seek after angels, nor should they pray to them. According to the Bible, they will obey and perform only the Lord's word. Even still, if we as believers were to believe God and expect God to utilize angelic ministry more often, it is most certain that in such an atmosphere of faith we would not only be more aware of their presence but also refreshingly experience their supernatural ministry more than ever.

Angelic ministry is all about faith and *expectation*. The truth is that if we do not expect God to do something, it probably won't happen. In Hebrews 11 the Bible says that faith and holy expectation are essential if we are to truly experience the substance and supernatural power of God in these days.

Now faith is the substance of things hoped for, the evidence of things not seen....But without faith it is impossible to please him: for he that cometh to God must believe that he is, and that he is a rewarder of them that diligently seek him.

(Hebrews 11:1, 6)

An Angelic "Fad"

Christian fiction has its place but not when it borders on *theological fantasia*. It's not proper to talk about biblical angelic characters and cast them in imaginary roles. This has the potential of confusing the truth of Scripture with a Christian fiction writer's imagination, thus changing the raw meaning of God's Word. There is spiritual danger in this.

There has been a tremendous amount written about angels in the past several years. Some of it is outright error and New Age thought. But there have also been many informative books written from a Christian viewpoint. Although some of these Christian books are very informative and edifying, I thought it would be a good time to write about angels from a *new and fresh perspective*. You see, angels are not simply the stuff of children's cartoons, or a prime time TV series! It's time for you and I as believers to begin to experience more than ever their supernatural ministry!

Most books and manuals that teach about angels are primarily concerned with their characteristics, names, titles, classifications, and purposes—sometimes erroneously. For example, one well-known author has recently stated that according to the Bible, there is in fact no "angel song" because it is his belief that they do not sing at all! There are others who also have promoted some false conceptions of the nature and character of angels, which I hope this book will correct.

I think by now many in the church have (at least intellectually speaking) become thoroughly acquainted with angels—who they are and what they do. Although some of their characteristics will also be mentioned here, it has been my desire to talk more about *angelic dynamics*—not only how they interact with the Lord but also how they interact with the church in this late hour.

How to Hear the Angels Sing (and Not Be Deceived!)

Down through the ages, too many well-meaning Christians have been deceived by the enemy into listening to the wrong voices in their quest to understand the realm of heaven and its angels.

> *There are, it may be, so many kinds of voices in the world, and none of them is without signification.*
> (1 Corinthians 14:10–11)

> *Beloved, believe not every spirit, but try the spirits whether they are of God: because many false prophets are gone out into the world. Hereby know ye the Spirit of God: every spirit that confesseth that Jesus Christ is come in the flesh is of God.*
> (1 John 4:1–2)

Avoiding Deception

> *I marvel that ye are so soon removed from him that called you into the grace of Christ unto another gospel: which is not another; but there be some that trouble you, and would pervert the gospel of Christ. But though we, or an angel from heaven, preach any other gospel unto you than that which we have preached unto*

ANGELIC DYNAMICS

you, let him be accursed.

(Galatians 1:6–8)

But how do you protect yourself from hearing false voices? How do you know when you're truly hearing the angel song? God is faithful and will protect His own. He is the Good Shepherd.

My sheep hear my voice, and I know them, and they follow me.

(John 10:27)

When a child of God sincerely seeks the Good Shepherd and humbly prays to the Lord, the Holy Spirit will protect him from false voices. The Holy Spirit of Truth will shield God's people from deception when they seek the Lord. God has provided the means where one can insulate him or herself from being spiritually deceived.

The most important thing a Christian can do in avoiding deception is to simply stick to the Scriptures. But the condition of our hearts (for example, possessing the character qualities of humility and teachableness) is also another extremely important aspect in preventing deception.

The Conditions of Angelic Ministry

There's too much easy believism and conditionless promise mongering in the preaching today. There is too much unconditional teaching regarding the promises of God and angelic ministry. As with all biblical blessings and precious promises, there are *conditional* aspects to receiving them.

The angel of the Lord encampeth round about them that **fear him**, *and delivereth them.* (Psalm 34:7, emphasis added)

In other words, the Lord is warning us that there is simply no angelic protection guaranteed to those who choose the evil path.

For that they hated knowledge, and did not choose the fear of the Lord: they would none of my counsel: they despised all my reproof. Therefore shall they eat of the fruit of their own way, and be filled with their own devices.

(Proverbs 1:29–31)

The Bible is clear that there is no *good* "destiny" for anyone who doesn't fear God and who habitually and unashamedly enjoys worldliness and sin—regardless of how many promises they claim.

> *The secret of the LORD is with them that fear him; and he will show them his covenant.* (Psalm 25:14)

The angels of the Lord can carry blessings or curses to the people of God. It all depends on whether a professed believer is yielded and obedient to the Word of the Lord.

> *The LORD shall open unto thee his good treasure, the heaven to give the rain unto thy land in his season, and to bless all the work of thine hand: and thou shalt lend unto many nations, and thou shalt not borrow. And the LORD shall make thee the head, and not the tail; and thou shalt be above only, and thou shalt not be beneath; if that thou hearken unto the commandments of the LORD thy God, which I command thee this day, to observe and to do them: and thou shalt not go aside*

> *from any of the words which I command thee this day, to the right hand, or to the left, to go after other gods to serve them. But it shall come to pass, if thou wilt not hearken unto the voice of the LORD thy God, to observe to do all his commandments and his statutes which I command thee this day; that all these curses shall come upon thee, and overtake thee.*
> (Deuteronomy 28:12–15)

What is important here is that we come to understand the *conditions* in which God sends forth His angels and also discuss how actively they will be involved in the coming, end-time revival. It is important that we understand these conditions because God and His angels are holy. Depending on our heart attitudes, angels can bring forth blessings or judgment. It is my belief that our response, both individually and corporately, will directly impact the level of angelic activity on behalf of the church. It is incumbent upon us, therefore, to walk in the commands of Christ and in holiness, forgiveness, and faith so that believers experience what

God has intended for us all along—to make the church triumphant.

By reading this book it is our hope and prayer that you will realize that the true angelic hosts of glory are alive, active, and doing well and are far more involved in our everyday lives than some might think. As believers, it's time for us to reconsider the role of God's angels in the church with a biblically accurate and refreshing perspective.

—Golden Altar Publishing

PART I

ANGELS, A FRESH PERSPECTIVE

Chapter One
The Purpose of Angels

The Importance of Angels

I think it's good to take a little time to meditate on the Word of God and to prayerfully consider our Lord, His angels, and the glory realm, which is the final destination of all true believers in the Lord Jesus Christ. I also think it wise to make inquiry into some of the more sublime aspects regarding the glorious creatures who dwell in the realm where God lives. This will do us much "earthly" good if we understand the fantastic role angels play in connecting the earthly realm to the glory realm.

Angels and God's Glory

The study of angels is, in fact, an inquiry into another aspect of the glory of God's presence in the world. There has been much written about angels but many questions still remain regarding their es-

sence, their role in the economy of God, and the *conditions* of their operation. The Bible is clear in all these matters, and it's my desire to go a little further in explaining the angels of God's glory in this series.

Angels Are the Heavenly Servants of God

Bless the LORD, ye his angels, that excel in strength, that do his commandments, hearkening unto the voice of his word.
(Psalm 103:20)

They are called angels based on *what they do* rather than what they look like.

Angels, Messengers from Heaven

The word *angel* is derived from the Greek word, *angelos*, which means *messenger*. The Hebrew equivalent to the Greek word *angelos* is the word *mal'ak* which also means messenger. There are over three hundred direct references to angels in the Bible, and many more references can be drawn if you include the term "heavenly hosts."

Praise ye the LORD. *Praise ye the* LORD
from the heavens: praise him in the heights.
Praise ye him, all his angels: praise ye him,
all his hosts. Praise ye him, sun and moon:
praise him, all ye stars of light.
> (Psalm 148:1–3, emphasis added)

Angels are called messengers because they deliver messages from God to man. (See Daniel 8:15–22; Luke 1:19, 26–35.) Angels confirm God's Word and appear to mankind in order to convey the will of God who sends them.

As we have said, God will often use angels to bring messages to men. On several occasions He has faithfully done so with our family. Angels, then and now, are continually active as God's ambassadors in carrying out His plan of redemption on the earth. Like us, angels are created beings.

For by him were all things created, that are
in heaven, and that are in earth, visible
and invisible, whether they be thrones, or
dominions, or principalities, or powers: all
things were created by him, and for him.
> (Colossians 1:16)

But they were created eons ago before the world was made!

Where wast thou when I laid the foun-
dations of the earth?...When the morning
stars sang together, and all the sons of
God shouted for joy? (Job 38:4, 7)

The purpose of the study of angels should lead true Christians to fear God and glorify the Lord Jesus Christ who created them to enforce and carry out His redemptive plan of salvation. Although God's beautiful and powerful angels are to be acknowledged, respected, studied, and even admired, Paul admonished us not to worship angels or to be overly fixated by their presence—especially like some in the New Age movement. (See Galatians 1:12; 2 Thessalonians 2:9–11.)

Let no man beguile you of your reward in
a voluntary humility and worshipping of
angels, intruding into those things which
he hath not seen, vainly puffed up by his
fleshly mind. (Colossians 2:18)

We are also warned not to receive any

THE WILL OF GOD

message from an angel that in any way contradicts Holy Scripture.

> But though we, or an angel from heaven, preach any other gospel unto you than that which we have preached unto you, let him be accursed. (Galatians 1:8)

Even the devil can transform himself into the appearance of a beautiful and powerful angel of light.

> And no marvel; for Satan himself is transformed into an angel of light.
> (2 Corinthians 11:14)

Angels, who are loyal to God, would never preach a false gospel to you. Regardless, we should be thankful that Paul has warned us that there are counterfeit, dark angels who only do us harm and prevent the true gospel from being preached. As Bible students, all of us should be careful not to tread lightly on this subject. However, after one encounters such a creature, one is awed beyond imagination at the power and glory of God.

One Mediator

Angels should never be prayed to. Angels go between heaven and earth as messengers are dispatched by the Lord. Remember, angels do not mediate between God and man. One should not call upon them to do such a thing. One should never try to talk directly to angels. The Bible says there is only one mediator between God and man—the man, Christ Jesus.

> For there is one God, and one mediator between God and men, the man Christ Jesus. (1 Timothy 2:5)

Beloved, remember this, in all things, Christ is above all.

> Which he wrought in Christ, when he raised him from the dead, and set him at his own right hand in the heavenly places, far above all principality, and power, and might, and dominion, and every name that is named, not only in this world, but also in that which is to come.
> (Ephesians 1:20-21)

Jesus sends His angels in request to

faith-filled prayers that confirm the Word. The angels of glory obey God's commandments, not ours.

> *Bless ye the LORD, all ye his hosts; ye ministers of his, that do his pleasure.*
>
> (Psalm 103:21)

It is perfectly scriptural for a believer to request or ask Jesus to send angels to help in time of need, but there is spiritual protocol. No one should think that they can personally command their own entourage of angels. Jesus is the King of angels and He rules over them.

> *I Jesus have sent mine angel to testify unto you these things in the churches. I am the root and the offspring of David, and the bright and morning star.*
>
> (Revelation 22:16)

The Appearance of Angels

Angels can manifest in various ways. Sometimes they can appear as a man or a woman "unawares." They can also appear as some of the created elements—such as wind or fire. Not all angels have wings. Some angels are very large and some angels are quite small and juvenile in appearance. Interestingly enough, angels can appear either masculine or *feminine*.

> *Then lifted I up mine eyes, and looked, and, behold, there came out two women, and the wind was in their wings; for they had wings like the wings of a stork: and they lifted up the ephah between the earth and the heaven.*
>
> (Zechariah 5:9, emphasis added)

After reading this Scripture, my own "macho" perspective of angels was eternally altered!

God Likes Diversity

This should not be such a difficult thing to comprehend. Although it is true that some liberal denominations and New Age religions (and even some colorful gift cards sold at organic food store chains) seem to solely describe angels as having a weak or overly effeminate appearance, this excessive viewpoint should not make a Christian back away from the possibility of diverse forms.

For example, we see that on earth God created mankind in various and diverse forms. He made them different sizes, shapes, and colors. He made them male and female—and in their life cycle, he made them to appear infant-like, child-like, as well as mature.

God loves variety in heaven as well as on earth. Conceiving of angels this way does not mean one has become some sort of a prayerless wimp who is no longer capable of warring against the evil minions of hell. Jesus did say that in heaven there would be neither male nor female but some form of a higher celestial race that lives on a higher plane of existence. But that does not necessitate that all angels on heaven and in earth must look male!

Infantile Concepts

When the angels appeared to the shepherds, they weren't trembling in the fear of the Lord because they saw a bunch of fat little babies in diapers! What they must have seen is an awesome display of God's power and beauty through angelic hosts who had been sent to them by the Lord.

Obviously the prophet Daniel and the apostle John saw angels of great power and stature. (See Daniel 10-11.) They understood the power of the Lord. If some in the church do not understand the power of the Lord, it is because they are happy with their weak, Gerber baby image! An infantile, worldly, and backslidden church is a weak church that will not pray or fast for the saving of lost souls. A prayerless church refuses to war against the evil spirits and principalities that are arrayed against it. (See Ephesians 6:8-12.) This type of church is not the true church of the Holy Father and His glorious angels.

Though some medieval artists conceived of angels simply as overweight little babies with stubby wings, such stereotypical images should not water down the truth that God's angels in fact appear in a variety of forms and appearances.

The "Feminine" Stereotype

When we contemplate angels, we must avoid the extremes. Jesus said that in heaven we would neither marry nor be given in marriage but would be of a higher order of creatures—much like the angels. When New Age artists, painters, and authors solely depict angels as slightly built, female creatures, this is error as well. The fact that even though God's angels exist in the feminine form, so too, many of God's angels are extremely powerful and masculine in appearance. In the book of Revelation, the stratospherically tall angel was tall enough to reach up and touch the sun!

When angels are mentioned in the Bible, they are mentioned with masculine names such as Michael and Gabriel. In the Hebrew language, their names are written in the masculine gender most probably in order to denote strength, power, and authority. But this fact alone does not preclude the possibility that there are classes of angels that exist in the form of women, or children. Regardless, one only has to look around the creation of God's earth to see that the Lord loves physical forms and has chosen to express Himself in this way.

We can see also in the Scriptures that both cherubim and seraphim can have wings. (See Isaiah 6:1-7.) Some have two wings while others have four and still others have up to six wings! They have multiple vocations, offices, and giftings. They dress differently. As with human beings, each angel has its own individual appearance and personality. However, their appearance and personalities are perfect and lovely—beyond earthly description.

No doubt, angels can take on the appearance of men. This is why in Hebrews 13:2, Paul warned us to be hospitable and kind to others, since we may in fact be actually "entertaining" angels unawares! Angels can also appear as wind or fire. (See Psalm 104:4; Hebrews 1:7.)

"Lampas" Shekinah Angels

The Shekinah cloud of God was illuminated with the very light rays and beams of God's radiated glory. When one enters this Shekinah cloud, one cannot help but have this brilliant, heavenly substance imparted into them. As it caused Moses' face to shine brilliantly, likewise, it will cause yours to shine if you will enter God's Shekinah presence.

> *And it came to pass, when Moses came down from mount Sinai with the two tables of testimony in Moses' hand, when he came down from the mount, that Moses wist not that the skin of his face shone while he talked with him.*
>
> (Exodus 34:29)

> *But if the ministration of death, written and engraven in stones, was glorious, so that the children of Israel could not stedfastly behold the face of Moses for the glory of his countenance; which glory was to be done away.* (2 Corinthians 3:7)

> *And all that sat in the council, looking stedfastly on him, saw his face as it had been the face of an angel.* (Acts 6:15)

The reason angels pulsate and emanate so much light when they appear to man is that they have recently been in the glorious presence of God, beholding the face of God. And they carry some of this Shekinah glory with them when they come to earth.

Lamps of Celestial Light

The English word for *lamp* comes from the Greek word *lampos*, which was derived from the Hebrew word *niyr*, meaning *angel*. (The original meaning of the word *lampo* is "lamp, flaming beam, light, torch, radiant, magnificent in appearance, bright, clear, goodly, gorgeous, white, brilliant, brightness, to radiate with beams, etc.") In other words, angels are *luminescent creatures*. When the ancients like Abraham, Isaac, Jacob, and Manoah saw them they described them as "lighted lamps" in the original Hebrew.

When my wife, Anne, saw an angel, she recounted to me how the angel's robes appeared like fiery "glory beads" (or that they looked like an infinite number of finely connected *living diamonds*, which were interwoven with beautiful platinum-like threads, all of which were lighted like a lampshade with the glory of God), this brought home the meaning of the word *lampos*.

Angelic Transparency

You see, moral purity resident in an angel's heart is of such high spiritual quality (and is so transcendent compared to sinful man) that the internal attributes of an angel's "heart life" will actually shine forth the Shekinah through the face and countenance. This is why some angels' faces are described as appearing "like the sun." The Shekinah that was upon the angel that my wife encountered also seemed to be alive and effulgent with the very life of God! But unlike sunlight, this was soft light, yet at the same time it was brilliant, incandescent, lustrous, refulgent, and shiny. It was a like a "cool" laser beam, which, although brilliant, was not hard or hurtful to look upon. My wife did not need to squint nor did she need to don sunglasses!

And after these things I saw another angel come down from heaven, having great power; and the earth was lightened with his glory.

(Revelation 18:1, emphasis added)

None of us as believers on earth have been rewired or have been recreated physically in this realm into a superior or angelic substance—yet! But I believe during the millennium, certain yielded and humble believers will be endowed with powers that will surpass that of even the angels.

Then shall the righteous shine forth as the sun in the kingdom of their Father. Who hath ears to hear, let him hear.

(Matthew 13:43)

Because angels can travel faster than the speed of light and are able to pivot/translate from one dimension to the other; because they are endued with great strength, power, and wisdom and are perfect and beautiful; because they are sinless and pure of heart and countenance, mankind is considered to be created a "little lower" than them.

Thou madest him a little lower than the angels; thou crownedst him with glory and honour, and didst set him over the works of thy hands. (Hebrews 2:7)

This is why God refers to pre-regenerate mankind as a little lower than the angels. When my wife was visited by an angel, she described him as being brilliantly lit like a lampshade. His face was as pure as the noonday sun. In the garden of Eden, we too had the ability to shine like an angel. But since the fall, we have lost the ability to illuminate God's light and glory from original sin. But through Jesus Christ, we can reclaim lost glory and become a son of God higher than the angels! What grace!

And I saw another mighty angel come down from heaven, clothed with a cloud: and a rainbow was upon his head, and his face was as it were the sun, and his feet as pillars of fire. (Revelation 10:1)

Personal Encounters

In fact, when my wife encountered the large angel in our home some time ago, the two vivid details I remember most are the description of the angel's chiseled, noble profile and his glorious countenance. In addition, the angel's bright, glowing garments seem to be made of a fine, translucent, bead-like, shimmery material that reflected the living Shekinah light of God's presence. The revelation of the power of these beings hit her with great fear and trembling especially as she began to realize that this angel had just come fresh from the presence of God Almighty! This is our destiny as well! The throne of God!

There's only so much one can say in human language to describe these beings! And yet, even the lowliest regenerate born-again believer in Jesus Christ will be exalted above angels as Sons of the living God and joint heirs with Jesus Christ! (See 1 Peter 2:9.) This is real power! *This is true glory!*

Higher than the Angels

Jesus in His glorified form is of much higher brilliance, beauty, and power than any of the angels.

> *Being made so much better than the angels, as he hath by inheritance obtained a more excellent name than they.*
>
> (Hebrews 1:4)

Beyond the veil, the sons and daughters of the most High God will be perfectly transformed and will take on glorious new bodies of light. They will become a celestial race of royal kin and will rule and reign with the Lord Himself. We shall be joint-heirs of Jesus Christ and will even be exalted above the angels! In Christ, even the "lowest" believer has already been (legally and positionally speaking) exalted above the angels and is seated in heavenly places with Christ Jesus. (See Ephesians 2:1-8.)

So Much Better Than the Angels?

Sometimes, with all of life's vicissitudes, it seems hard to imagine that one day our faces will shine like the sun in the kingdom of our God! But the Bible says that even now we as believers in Christ have been legally and spiritually seated in heavenly places, far above all principalities and powers with Christ Jesus. (See Ephesians 2:6.) It is true that for those who continually abide in Christ, they have even now ascended and are seated in a place of spiritual authority with Jesus. According to Paul, we are already in that position in this church age even though we have not attained our glorified form and substance until we have shed these bodies and put on immortality. (See Romans 8:20-23.)

Heavenly, Angelic "Fashion"

Many of heaven's angels are dressed in seamless robes of pure white while others dress in a variety of differently colored garments. The angel who rolled away the stone from our Lord's tomb appeared like "lightening" to those in the garden that Easter morning. (See Matthew 28:1-4.) In Acts 1:9-11 two angels who were "dressed in white clothing" appeared to the disciples after the resurrection and stood nearby while Jesus ascended into heaven.

Angels have various characteristics. *They are as unique in their appearance as people are!* Each of their faces is unique and perfect and, though different, one is not more beautiful than the others. And there is no way to describe the kind countenance and sweet smile that are on the angels' faces.

In the new celestial Eden there are trees bearing the most delicious fruit. In heaven, there are pristine vistas and views of the most beautiful flowers of every color and hue sending forth aromas of surpassing fragrances. Birds of glorious plumage even now are singing their carols of joy and pure praise unto God in a new world where the lion lays down with the lamb.

Angelic Encounters

First Angelic Encounter

When my wife came to me one day and told me she had seen an angel, I was totally fascinated. This experience reminded me of a man named Manoah who lived in Israel during the time of the judges.

His wife came to him and also told him that she had seen an angel.

And there was a certain man of Zorah, of the family of the Danites, whose name was Manoah; and his wife was barren and had borne no children. Then the angel of the LORD appeared to the woman, and said to her, "Behold now, you are barren and have borne no children, but you shall conceive and give birth to a son. Now therefore, be careful not to drink wine or strong drink, nor eat any unclean thing."...Then the woman came and told her husband, saying, "A man of God came to me and his appearance was like the appearance of the angel of God, very awesome. And I did not ask him where he came from, nor did he tell me his name."

(Judges 13:2-4, 6 NASB)

I can't exactly say how the Old Testament prophet Manoah must have felt when his wife told him she had seen an angel, but I know I responded the same way he did, for I told her how much I would like to see an angel as well!

> *Then Manoah entreated the LORD, and said, O my Lord, let the man of God which thou didst send come again unto us, and teach us what we shall do unto the child that shall be born. And God hearkened to the voice of Manoah; and the angel of God came again unto the woman as she sat in the field: but Manoah her husband was not with her.*
>
> (Judges 13:8-9)

When Manoah's wife came to him that day and told him she had been visited by an angel, his life would never be the same again, for he too would experience the ministry of angels in a very direct and beautiful manner.

> *So Manoah took a kid with a meat offering, and offered it upon a rock unto the LORD: and the angel did wondrously; and Manoah and his wife looked on. For it came to pass, when the flame went up toward heaven from off the altar, that the angel of the LORD ascended in the flame of the altar. And Manoah and his wife looked on it, and fell on their faces to the ground.*   (Judges 13:19-20)

Whether Manoah saw the pre-incarnate Christ, or whether it was a powerful messenger angel from on high, his wife's testimony impacted him greatly and created hunger in his life for more of the supernatural, manifest presence of God. My wife's testimony greatly encouraged me to seek God for a supernatural encounter which God later granted and which would birth out of His Spirit the entire *Song of Angels* project. I wasn't a songwriter by trade, but God still supernaturally provided the music necessary to communicate the message He had put upon my heart.

How Hungry Are You?

Are you hungry to encounter God? Are you desperately searching for a fresh place in His presence? Do you truly believe in angels? And if you do, are you open to their ministry on behalf of the Lord? We see the results of Manoah's spiritual hunger and his desire to sacrifice unto the Lord, His God. We see this gave him an even greater vision of God's glory and a clearer understanding of God's plans and

purposes for his life on earth. For his wife was about to give birth to a mighty man of valor—a champion of Israel who the Philistines would fear.

Because my wife, Anne, prays, fasts, and gives to the poor so often, I believe this is one of the reasons God visited her one day in a special way. In her life, it's not about seeking after angels or anything else from the Lord. It's all about seeking Jesus. Her hunger for Christ and her own testimony challenged me and forever changed my perspective on angels in general. And there are times when simply observing the private devotional life of your spouse or another dedicated believer can spark real spiritual passion within you and challenge you to seek God more earnestly.

Like Manoah, I wanted the reality of His presence that his wife had experienced regarding God's ministers of fire. And God has not disappointed me.

Angels and Ordinary People

Angelic visitations and ministry are not just the stuff of Old Testament seers or first century apostles. *Angels are for everyone!*

Cornelius was an ordinary man who had an extraordinary encounter with one of God's messenger angels. He loved to pray, fast, and give alms as well.

> *There was a certain man in Caesarea called Cornelius, a centurion of the band called the Italian band....He saw in a vision evidently about the ninth hour of the day an angel of God coming in to him, and saying unto him, Cornelius. And when he looked on him, he was afraid, and said, What is it, Lord? And he said unto him, Thy prayers and thine alms are come up for a memorial before God.*
> (Acts 10:1, 3–4)

As I mentioned briefly earlier, several years ago, while praying late one evening, my wife, Anne, had a face-to-face encounter with a very strong, powerful, large, and exceptionally beautiful eight-foot tall angel. Believe me, my wife and I are very practical and ordinary people. Why God chose that point in our lives to visit my wife is still a mystery to us. Evidently God had sent him to visit our home to encourage Anne after she had just concluded an extended seven-day period of fasting and prayer for a young neighbor child who needed salvation and whose home life was desperate.

A Vivid Encounter

Her description of the angel's appearance was so vivid and fascinating to me! Several years later on Christmas Eve, God granted me a vision of angels by His sovereign grace—a veritable celestial odyssey that I sing about on this album and write about in this book. But these experiences do not make any of us think that we are now "special." As a matter of fact, having such experiences has only made us more *accountable* to God!

The Final Frontier

Sooner or later angels will be your main transport to the glory realm.

And it came to pass, that the beggar died, and was carried by the angels.
(Luke 16:22)

Only a fiery transport driven by an angelic charioteer from heaven can take any of us to where all Christians long to be sooner or later. The Lord of Glory Himself flies on the wings of cherubim.

He bowed the heavens also, and came down; and darkness was under his feet. And he rode upon a cherub, and did fly: and he was seen upon the wings of the wind.
(2 Samuel 22:10–11)

Indeed, glory is the "final frontier" for all who choose Christ as Lord and Savior. And the final frontier will not be discovered by Star Trek *Enterprise* or by any other imaginary space explorer! It is only through the power of the risen Christ that we can advance toward our final destination. It is only by the power of the Holy Spirit and with angelic aid that we may dwell in the glory realm.

The Bible tells us the future of the redeemed is the third heaven. (See 2 Corinthians 12:2; John 14:2.) This is the future home for all God's elect. It is an actual place where there exists the Celestial City of God, called the New Jerusalem. And only a fiery chariot of angels can take you there—no spaceship on earth will ever be able to accomplish this!

The Vault of Heaven

God is about to unveil some glorious hidden truths to His people in this hour regarding heaven, prophecy, and increased angelic activities on planet earth. The Lord wants you to know there is great and lasting wealth in heaven, which adds no sorrow and which endures forever. (See Proverbs 10:22.) Some of this heavenly wealth is about to be transferred by happy angels to true believers in order to bring in the harvest of the nations.

True ministers of the gospel are now beginning to train their people how to war against the devil and the spirit of poverty. The spirit of reformation is "in the air" and angelic activity is ever increasing. God's heavenly vault has now been opened and the treasures and revelation of His glory are about to be bestowed on all who will seek it.

Resources to Preach

In order that world missions be thoroughly accomplished, individual Christians and corporate ministries must have the resources to accomplish the final task. The angels of heaven know that when every nation has heard the Word of the gospel, then the end will come, and the new reign of Christ will begin. And, the angels are busy trying to prepare the earth for the coming of the Messiah.

And this gospel of the kingdom shall be preached in all the world for a witness unto all nations; and then shall the end come. (Matthew 24:14)

And he shall send his angels with a great sound of a trumpet, and they shall gather together his elect from the four winds, from one end of heaven to the other.
(Matthew 24:31)

My friend, be patient in the Holy Spirit. God and His angels are on your side. Jesus loves you very much! Trust God that He will cause the vision of abundance He has already given to come to pass. Pray, work hard, and persevere. Commit all your ways to Him. Tithe and be a cheerful giver. God will bring wealth from the four corners of the earth to your very doorstep!

> *Give, and it will be given to you: good measure, pressed down, shaken together, and running over will be put into your bosom. For with the same measure that you use, it will be measured back to you.*
>
> (Luke 6:38 NKJV)

There are literally acres of diamonds within your reach. And if you have troubles, rejoice! The time of your reward is nigh.

> *And to you who are troubled rest with us, when the Lord Jesus shall be revealed from heaven with his mighty angels.*
>
> (2 Thessalonians 1:7)

As you begin to tithe and trust God with your finances, the angels of the Lord will literally bring the wealth of this planet to you and your family.

The Enduring Wealth of Heaven

God and His mighty angels want you to realize that the gold people cherish, the jewels they adore, the cities and mansions that are built in this world, are only paltry, distant copies of the real city that is soon coming down from heaven. If God can make the universe, why does anyone doubt His ability to suspend a city in the sky beyond the stars?

And oh, what a reception there will be in heaven—there will be no beggarly reception there! What a day! And what a celestial promenade there will be! I have heard accounts of how the servant, Moses, himself, will charioteer many of the redeemed on a flaming golden chariot. He and other great saints will actually take the "new arrivals" on a tour of the Celestial City! And what a glorious heavenly parade there will be! What a day that will be! In heaven, the one-time, offscourings of the earth will be welcomed as kings by angelic hosts. These are the future rulers of the new heaven and earth.

> Blessed are the meek: for they shall inherit the earth....Rejoice, and be exceeding glad: for great is your reward in heaven.
> (Matthew 5:5, 12)

> His lord said unto him, Well done, thou good and faithful servant: thou hast been faithful over a few things, I will make thee ruler over many things: enter thou into the joy of thy lord....His lord said unto him, Well done, good and faithful servant; thou hast been faithful over a few things, I will make thee ruler over many things: enter thou into the joy of thy lord.
> (Matthew 25:21, 23)

In our glorified state in heaven, even the lowliest Christian from earth will be raised above the angelic powers.

> Do ye not know that the saints shall judge the world? And if the world shall be judged by you, are ye unworthy to judge the smallest matters? **Know ye not that we shall judge angels?** How much more things that pertain to this life? (1 Corinthians 6:2–3, emphasis added)

> For unto the angels hath he not put in subjection the world to come, whereof we speak. (Hebrews 2:5)

> For he did not put the world to come, about which we are speaking, under the control of angels. (Hebrews 2:5 NET)

Angels inside the Gates

Heaven is alive and is an immense and abundant place full of happy angelic hosts. Hasn't our Savior promised a kingdom where the weakest and humblest of His children will rule and reign with Him, the King of Kings and the Lord of Lords? The Bible says that all true believers shall rule with Christ for all the ages (*aeons*) to come!

I urge you to give your immediate difficulties and trials to the Lord for they will distract you from experiencing His presence and from getting heavenly discernment. Rather than focusing on such distractions, get on your face before God and worship Him until He comes to you so that you, too, will catch a fresh vision of glory.

You need to forget the old and press on into the new! For, by faith, our souls will soon leave this world and will rise upwards and will pass through the gates and into the city! Out of the earth and out of the old body! Out of the mortal into the immortal! Out of death into life! Out of the old into the new! For new life eternal lies ahead and above, inside the gates. An eternal crystal sea, with fire mingled throughout, glittering as far as the eye can see! Angels, angels, angels everywhere! The song of angels everywhere! Angels will be heard talking, singing, and rejoicing. Angels will be heard playing instruments and blowing trumpets. Angels will be dancing and praising the King. Such a scene no mortal ever saw! Such floods of inner joy will flood the whole being when one catches a vision of their eternal destiny.

But ye are come unto mount Sion, and unto the city of the living God, the heavenly Jerusalem, and to an innumerable company of angels. (Hebrews 12:22)

The heavens are filled with happy angels who are ready to escort the children of the king throughout the Celestial City. Angels will walk with you there. The angels will talk with you there and will explain the meaning of things, which before you could never have comprehended. We will all hear the angels' heavenly song and we will be taught a new song that now only the angels enjoy. However, even the angels won't be able to sing our new song of redemption to the Lamb!

It's hard to imagine that one day soon we will all surpass the angels with our own song of triumphant worship! And the angels will hear the new song of the redeemed! Then all of us will join in with the angelic choirs in a sight not to be forgotten! Millions of transparent souls will stand and shout and dance for joy on that Crystal Sea! And God has appointed angels to protect and guide you and your family on this earth. God wants your journey to heaven to be a blessed one!

For he shall give his angels charge over thee, to keep thee in all thy ways. (Psalm 91:11)

Our heavenly Father longs to show you what He has prepared for those that love Jesus! (See 1 Corinthians 2:10; Revelation 3:21.) Our final destination is not of this world. Our citizenship is in heaven. Our life work and service on earth, our hardships and trials, are only brief and passing incidents on the way to eternal life. Consider the current trials and tribulations of your life tests that prepare the eternal weight of God's glory in you. (See 2 Corinthians 3:18; 4:6, 17.)

For which cause we faint not; but though our outward man perish, yet the inward man is renewed day by day. For our light affliction, which is but for a moment, worketh for us a far more exceeding and eternal weight of glory; while we look not at the things which are seen, but at the things which are not seen: for the things which are seen are temporal; but the things which are not seen are eternal.

(2 Corinthians 4:16–18)

Chapter Two
Angels in Our Midst

Many people ask if they have a guardian angel. The Bible infers that every true believer in Christ has a guardian angel and also has multiple angels to guide them through the vicissitudes of life.

And they said unto her, Thou art mad. But she constantly affirmed that it was even so. Then said they, It is his angel.

(Acts 12:15)

It is obvious that the early church believed in "personal" angels.

Every child has a ministry of angels. The angels of children have constant access to the throne of God in heaven. They always behold the face of the Father.

Take heed that ye despise not one of these little ones; for I say unto you, That in heaven their angels do always behold the face of my Father which is in heaven.

(Matthew 18:10)

And if someone has lost a young child, be assured that it was that same angel that carried that child with him to paradise with great joy!

The righteous perisheth, and no man layeth it to heart: and merciful men are taken away, none considering that the righteous is taken away from the evil to come.

(Isaiah 57:1)

Corporately speaking, it appears that every true New Testament believing church on earth has a special angel that protects and ministers to that particular body of believers.

The mystery of the seven stars that you saw in my right hand and the seven golden lampstands is this: the seven stars are the angels of the seven churches and the seven lampstands are the seven churches. "To the angel of the church in Ephesus, write the following: 'This is the solemn pronouncement of the One who has a firm grasp on the seven stars in his right hand—the One who walks among the seven golden lampstands.'"

(Revelation 1:20; 2:1 NET)

As a matter of fact, every saved person has angels present to minister to them.

> *Are they not all ministering spirits, sent forth to minister for them who shall be heirs of salvation?*   (Hebrews 1:14)

Angels see us in our struggles and assist us when we comply and obey the Word of God. Even though most believers seldom see angels, this does not mean they aren't present and aren't actively helping them in their work for Christ.

> *Who maketh his angels spirits; his ministers a flaming fire.*   (Psalm 104:4)

And even though many never actually see one, don't ever forget, my friend, they are always watching over all of us.

> *For I think that God hath set forth us the apostles last, as it were appointed to death: for we are made a spectacle...and to angels...*   (1 Corinthians 4:9)

To those who may be skeptical, may I say this—whether you believe in the ministry of angels or not, your life has most likely already been protected and assist-ed by angelic hosts *many times*. Most all of you have already enjoyed frequent angelic interventions in your lives for the good, even if you have not been aware of them.

> *Let brotherly love continue. Be not forgetful to entertain strangers: for thereby some have entertained angels unawares.*
>   (Hebrews 13:1–2)

The Messengers of Glory

Angels are referenced to in the Scriptures as the "*kadoshim*" (meaning the holy ones).

> *And the angel answering said unto him, I am Gabriel, that stand in the presence of God.*   (Luke 1:19)

Angels are created beings from the glory realm. The glory realm or heaven is the home of both God and His angels. As we live more purely and pray more fervently we become spiritually attuned and more aware of this glory realm. As a direct result of our increased spiritual cognizance, we become more aware of angelic operations in our daily lives. Angels carry with them a message of God and can preach the gospel.

Angels have many different functions in relation to the end-time church. In fact, the message of the *Song of Angels* is very much about another aspect of the manifest presence of a holy God and the holy nature of God whom angels worship. In other words, if we could catch one note of their pure song of worship, we would have a holy frustration with some of the earthy worship and praise we participate in today.

Angelic Yearnings

I feel a sense of urgency to leave my listeners with what I feel is a "message" from the Holy Spirit that began with the vision of these angels. The supreme desire of all angels and the core of their message is to exalt Christ as Lord and Savior and to assist in the proclamation of the gospel of salvation to the lost.

The Fallen Cherubs' Role

God wastes nothing. The devil's rebellion with a third of the angels would somehow work within the economy of God. Even Satan himself ultimately works toward God's sovereign purposes.

Now there was a day when the sons of God came to present themselves before the LORD, and Satan came also among them... and the LORD said unto Satan, Whence comest thou? Then Satan answered the LORD, and said, From going to and fro in the earth, and from walking up and down in it....Then Satan answered the LORD, and said, Doth Job fear God for nought?... And the LORD said unto Satan, Behold, all that he hath is in thy power; only upon himself put not forth thine hand. So Satan went forth from the presence of the LORD.

(Job 1:6–7, 9, 12)

And Satan stood up against Israel, and provoked David to number Israel.

(1 Chronicles 21:1)

God is in control over all and has given believers authority in His name because even the devil is used to accomplish the Lord's will in causing His chosen people to learn to overcome. In order to master the enemy, however, it is necessary that men and women of God engage in spiritual warfare and pray to the Lord Jesus Christ for angelic intervention in their lives and ministry. There is a real enemy to overcome out there.

The thief cometh not, but for to steal, and to kill, and to destroy: I am come that they might have life, and that they might have it more abundantly. (John 10:10)

As a matter of fact, life in this world is a training ground for the *"spirits of just men [and women] made perfect"* (Hebrews 12:23); it is on-the-job training in overcoming the devil and his evil minions—and we need God's angels to help us. When we learn how to abide in the Word and to practice God's presence, when we understand the power of His blood and the ministry of His angels, we will be able to pull down every stronghold of the enemy.

I have written unto you, young men, because ye are strong, and the word of God abideth in you, and ye have overcome the wicked one. (1 John 2:14)

Angels confirm God's Word and appear to mankind in order to convey the will of God who sends them. Angels also assist us in prophecy as well as in preaching and are present in church services that are flowing in God's Holy Spirit.

But every woman that prayeth or prophesieth....For this cause ought the woman to have power on her head because of the angels. (1 Corinthians 11:5, 10)

"Effortless" Evangelism

One thing is for sure, no believer should ever become overly concerned if they have seen an angel. Besides, there are many who have entertained angels *unawares* and one can show up that another may see even if you don't!

For example, one evening I was preaching at a large congregation in New Hampshire when a man (who happened to be an unsaved, well-educated, well-mannered, and prominent Bostonian attorney) stood up in the meeting, trembling and crying. He exclaimed that while I was prophesying, he could see a large, bright, white angel touching my tongue as I was speaking. Needless to say, this gentleman got born again and baptized in the Holy Spirit after the service!

A Solemn Word

Later that night in our hotel room, God told me that if we were to walk in any sin or pride in our ministry, He would immediately withdraw not only His presence but the presence of angels as well. He also said that he had appointed a particular "power" angel to help us in our ministry, and we would know when he shows up because things would begin to happen! Souls would be saved and filled with the Holy Spirit, bodies would be healed, emotions and minds would be healed, demons would be cast out, the blind would see, and the lame would walk, and the glory of God would be upon the worship. Then folks would get a vision for their specific calling in Christ. After getting this vision, it would be so much easier to challenge so many to fulfill the call upon their lives and for some to enter the mission field.

Angelic Vision

In Genesis 12:1-3, God visited Abraham and gave him the very first great commission found in the Bible. After God had supernaturally shown Abraham the stars of the heavens would be as his offspring, it was easy for Abraham to answer the call. With angelic help and heavenly intervention, evangelism will become a much easier task for all of us! Angels aren't only partners of prophets, but they are also partners of all the saints in Christ.

There are many other instances in the Bible when angels showed up to "partner up" with believers in order to help them in time of need. (See, for example, Lot, Genesis 19:17, 29; Moses, Exodus 33:1-2; Elijah, 1 Kings 19:2-8; all the saints, Psalm 78:23; Jesus, Luke 22:43; Philip, Acts 8:26; Paul, Acts 27:23-24.)

The Angels of Mamre

And the LORD appeared unto him in the plains of Mamre: and he sat in the tent door in the heat of the day; and he lift up his eyes and looked, and, lo, three men stood by him: and when he saw them, he ran to meet them from the tent door, and bowed himself toward the ground.

(Genesis 18:1–2)

The Lord and His angels appeared to Abraham amongst the trees in Mamre in order to confirm the prophetic word given to Abraham that Sarah would bear him a child. Shortly thereafter, those same angels destroyed Sodom and Gomorrah for refusing to obey the righteous word of the Lord.

Don't Get an Angel Angry!

The two angels arrived at Sodom in the evening, and Lot was sitting in the gateway of the city. When he saw them, he got up to meet them and bowed down with his face to the ground....Before they had gone to bed, all the men from every part of the city of Sodom—both young and old—sur-rounded the house. They called to Lot, "Where are the men who came to you tonight? Bring them out to us so that we can have sex with them."(Genesis 19:1, 4–5 NIV)

The angels assisted Abraham in proclaiming the word of the Lord to the wicked inhabitants of the ancient metropolis of Sodom and Gomorrah. Remember, angelic intervention is *conditional*. When the homosexual and perverted citizens of Sodom attempted to rape one of the angels, God had had enough! The power that these angels exercised in the total destruction of these twin cities was greater than that of the most powerful nuclear bombs. When God withdraws His presence and His angels because of prolonged unrepentant sin, any person or nation faces extermination and eternal wrath! In short, angels don't hang out with habitual sinners. Nor will they stand by and protect a wicked nation for very long.

Righteousness exalteth a nation: but sin is a reproach to any people.

(Proverbs 14:34)

Various "Power" Angels

The angels of God are awesome and powerful. In the Bible they are called "mighty ones."

> And I saw another mighty angel come down from heaven, clothed with a cloud: and a rainbow was upon his head, and his face was as it were the sun, and his feet as pillars of fire: and he had in his hand a little book open: and he set his right foot upon the sea, and his left foot on the earth. (Revelation 10:1-2)

Some angels focus on worship while others attend God's throne. Some comprise God's army while others are involved in administrative duties. Cherubim and seraphim angels make memorable appearances in Ezekiel 1:4-28 and Isaiah 6:2-6. In Daniel 4:13, a certain class of angels is referred to as "watchers," meaning a "holy one come down over my bed." All of them are subject to Christ. (See 1 Peter 3:22.) The Bible is replete with examples of angels appearing to many men and women of God in both the Old and the New Testaments. To all of us who are covenant believers in Jesus Christ, we are entitled to the ministry of "power" angels. (See Hebrews 1:14.)

Angelic "Shock and Awe"

Angels excel in strength. In Isaiah 37:36, one angel killed 185,000 Assyrians. Throughout the Old Testament, the angels of God were always busy keeping the Israelites from being destroyed by their enemies.

> For I will defend this city to save it for mine own sake, and for my servant David's sake. Then the angel of the LORD went forth, and smote in the camp of the Assyrians a hundred and fourscore and five thousand. (Isaiah 37:35-36)

One thing is certain, angels hear your prayers and are sent by God to help you in your walk with Christ. (See Luke 1:13.) Even though you may not have barbarians, such as the evil Amalekites and Assyrians, physically attacking your home and ministry, there are certainly demons

attacking you and your loved ones! But they are no match for Jesus and His angels if we pray and take our rightful authority over them.

A Ministry of Love and Care

God loves you and me very, very much. God is your friend. He delights in you and is the best friend you'll ever have! The ministry of angels illustrates another aspect of God's love for His saints (by the way, I believe a "saint" is any genuine believer who has sincere faith in Jesus Christ and obeys Him). God is no respecter of persons. God wants to spare your home (see Acts 16:31) and save your life, even as He did for Paul in Acts.

For there stood by me this night the angel of God, whose I am, and whom I serve, Saying, Fear not, Paul; thou must be brought before Caesar: and, lo, God hath given thee all them that sail with thee.

(Acts 27:23-24)

I believe God sent an angel to cause an earthquake, which shook the very foundations of the prison where Paul was held prisoner. After the angel divinely intervened to rescue Paul from prison, notice the conversions that took place.

And suddenly there was a great earthquake, so that the foundations of the prison were shaken: and immediately all the doors were opened, and every one's bands were loosed. And the keeper of the prison awaking out of his sleep, and seeing the prison doors open, he drew out his sword, and would have killed himself, supposing that the prisoners had been fled....Then he called for a light, and sprang in, and came trembling, and fell down before Paul and Silas, and brought them out, and said, Sirs, what must I do to be saved?

(Acts 16:26-27, 29-30)

Again, evangelism becomes almost effortless when we allow God to express Himself supernaturally the way He desires to in our midst.

Unbelief puts God in a box, but our responsibility is to obey God with a pure heart and confess like Mary did, "May *everything you said come true"* (Luke 1:38 TLB).

Innumerable Angels

The amount of angels God has created is as "innumerable as the stars above." When Elijah was taken up into heaven, he was taken up by an angelic chariot of fire. (See 2 Kings 2:11–12.) The Bible says the fiery, angelic chariots of God are twenty thousand, thousands upon thousands and some Bible scholars estimate this to be approximately 100 trillion angels!

The chariots of God are twenty thousand, even thousands of thousands.
(Psalm 68:17 NKJV)

Scientists now tell us there are more stars in the universe than all the combined sand granules from all the oceans and beaches of this entire planet. And to think that there could very well be more angels than this!

As the host of heaven cannot be numbered, neither the sand of the sea measured.
(Jeremiah 33:22)

The prophet Jeremiah also said that the total number of angels is *innumerable.* Not even the largest computers ever built or that ever will be built will be able to count them. There are more than enough of them to protect and help every believer in his or her walk with the Lord.

Memorable Seraphic Quotes

I would like to quote the opinions regarding angels and their interactions with believers from more "recent prophets" of God in this church age.

Angels...have a greater influence on this world than men are generally aware of. We ought to admire the grace of God toward us sinful creatures in that He has appointed His holy angels to guard us against mischiefs of wicked spirits who are always intending our hurt both to our bodies and to our souls.

**—Increase Mather,
(the great Puritan preacher)**

The founder of the Salvation Army vividly described angels in the vision he had.

White and dazzling...every angel was surrounded with an aura of rainbows so brilliant, that were it not withheld, no human being could stand the sight of it.

—General William Booth

The angels act for God, for us and for themselves. For God: they reflect the great mercy with which He encompasses us...then for themselves: they eagerly desire to see us fill the places that were made empty in their ranks, for the lips of children, but lately fed with milk and not with solid food, are to perfect the choir destined to celebrate His divine majesty.

—St. Bernard

Angels beyond the Veil

There is a particular book of the Bible that clearly reveals how responsive angels are to a believer's fervent prayer. In the book of Zechariah (which I call the "angel's book" of the Bible), it was as if God chose to "peel back" the curtain in order to "un-shroud" the glory realm of angelic activity so that we could not only see how

angels minister to God but also how they minister on behalf of the saints.

And they answered the angel of the LORD that stood among the myrtle trees, and said, We have walked to and fro through the earth, and, behold, all the earth sitteth still, and is at rest. Then the angel of the LORD answered and said, O LORD of hosts, how long wilt thou not have mercy on Jerusalem and on the cities of Judah, against which thou hast had indignation these threescore and ten years? And the LORD answered the angel that talked with me with good words and comfortable words. So the angel that communed with me said unto me, Cry thou, saying, Thus saith the LORD of hosts; I am jealous for Jerusalem and for Zion with a great jealousy.

(Zechariah 1:11–14)

I will also gather all nations, and will bring them down into the valley of Jehoshaphat, and will plead with them there for my people and for my heritage Israel, whom they have scattered among the nations, and parted my land. (Joel 3:2)

It is important for both church and political leaders to understand the fact that God has sovereignly determined what the borders of Israel are to be in Ezekiel 47:15–21.

Any leader or nation who would deliberately cause the division of the land of Israel—anyone who would even attempt to change the borders that God has ordained (even under the guise of "land for peace") risks the wrath of God and will find themselves facing a legion of angels. These angels control everything from famine, plagues, and disease to hurricanes, tornadoes, tsunamis, floods, and earthquakes. (See Exodus 8–12; Revelation 8–10.)

Pro-Israeli Angels

God has said in His Word that Israel is the apple of His eye. (See Genesis 12:1–3; 13:14–17; 15:18; 17:7.) Remember, angels exist in order to perform God's Word.

Bless the LORD, ye his angels, that excel in strength, that do his commandments, hearkening unto the voice of his word.
(Psalm 103:20)

We know from God's Word that Michael the Archangel protects the nation of Israel. Although not in the Bible, many Jewish scholars believe that the Archangel Ariel also protects Israel. I cannot tell you how many times I have seen once-prosperous and flourishing ministries and nations literally go down the path of destruction by putting the nation of Israel on par with the gentile nations.

Sure, God is no respecter of persons. But the Bible says that He has a special plan and in revealing His Son through the tiny nation of Israel. Anyone who has a complaint with this needs to take it up with Michael and, according to Jewish scholars, Ariel. I for one do not want to find myself fighting the curse of God and the archangels of heaven!

And it shall come to pass in that day, that I will seek to destroy all the nations that come against Jerusalem.
(Zechariah 12:9)

No Land for "Peace"

Any person or nation that wittingly or unwittingly seeks to divide the land or in any way hurts the security and preservation of Israel will have to deal with the unseen, righteous forces of God's angelic Hosts.

> O ye seed of Israel his servant, ye children of Jacob, his chosen ones. He is the LORD our God; his judgments are in all the earth. Be ye mindful always of his covenant; the word which he commanded to a thousand generations; even of the covenant which he made with Abraham, and of his oath unto Isaac; and hath confirmed the same to Jacob for a law, and to Israel for an everlasting covenant, saying, Unto thee will I give the land of Canaan, the lot of your inheritance.
>
> (1 Chronicles 16:13–18)

This Scripture clearly reveals God's special plan for the nation of Israel in the end times. It also shows the influence angels have regarding this tiny nation's future destiny. Not only does this passage of Scripture show how the angels would disdain a doctrine such as "replacement theology," it also teaches us something about their supernatural activities regarding the church in this late hour.

Angelic Dynamics

As an illustration of such encounters with the celestial realm, consider that most dialogue in the book of Zechariah, recorded by the prophet, is either God speaking to angels, angels speaking to God, angels speaking to men, or men speaking to angels. As an example, the prophet heard and recorded angels talking to God (Zechariah 1:12–13), angels talking to each other (Zechariah 2:3–5), angels talking to the prophet (Zechariah 1:1), Zechariah talking back to the angels (Zechariah 1:19; 2:2), and, of course, the Lord speaking directly to Zechariah throughout the entire book! Zechariah sure had some glorious experiences in intercession and in his prayer time.

Angels for All Nations

And why shouldn't there be modern-day

Zechariahs in this hour? Why can't we have ministers under the new covenant that operate in the same angelic realm that Zechariah did? Why can't prophets and apostles in this day operate with at least as much power as the great old covenant prophets like Elijah and Zechariah? Apparently, they were very consecrated and anointed brothers. Yet, they were men of "like passion" who were made of the same mental and physical constitution as believers in the new covenant today.

Still, you may ask why these brothers and sisters experience in the Old Testament so much angelic activity. Some will attribute this to sheer "dispensationalism" but the Bible makes no such claim.

What was their spiritual secret to unlocking the supernatural realm of God? Possibly, they exercised their spirit man in the simplicity of intense intercession. Or maybe it was because they were more spiritually advanced in their sensitivity to the glory realm. In the soon to be released book, *Golden Altar™ Worship*, we have attempted to go into greater detail in explaining how a New Testament believer can begin to worship God more effectively by simply revisiting this old covenant "power zone."

Too many shy away from the supernatural realm because a few have abused such blessed doctrines. Because of this, many have put a "religious spin" on the subject relegating all such powers to the past. No matter what the reason, James, the brother of Jesus, said that the prophets of old were still made of the same "stuff" that we are.

> *Elias was a man subject to like passions as we are, and he prayed earnestly that it might not rain: and it rained not on the earth by the space of three years and six months.*
>
> (James 5:17)

God is no respecter of persons. (See Acts 10:34.) Zechariah was simply more focused in prayer and lived in the heavenlies—much more than the majority of the "high speed," modern day, high-tech believers today. He was a holy man, consecrated unto God—a man of great prayer and faith. Zechariah was not as distracted with many of the things that plague modern believers today.

Spiritual Dumbness

Of course there are spiritual repercussions whenever a believer discounts or questions God's plans or purposes administered through an angel. This is especially true if the angel has been sent from God to fulfill purpose in ministry and as long as the angelic messenger has not contradicted Scripture in any way. For instance, because Zacharias didn't immediately receive the ministry of Gabriel, he was stricken with temporary dumbness by the angel.

And the angel answering said unto him, I am Gabriel, that stand in the presence of God; and am sent to speak unto thee, and to show thee these glad tidings. And, behold, thou shalt be dumb, and not able to speak, until the day that these things shall be performed, because thou believest not my words, which shall be fulfilled in their season. And the people waited for Zacharias, and marvelled that he tarried so long in the temple. And when he came out, he could not speak unto them: and they perceived that he had seen a vision in the temple: for he beckoned unto them, and remained speechless.

(Luke 1:19–22)

All too often, many believers have been made spiritually "dumb" by their own unbelief in the capabilities of a supernatural God. *They are not able to speak to men for God because they have spent so little time speaking to God on behalf of men.* Sadly, because so many contemporary believers are full of unbelief and prayerlessness, Christianity has virtually become a religious form of entertainment or a pastime for some. For others, Christianity has become solely an intellectual exercise, whereby the will voluntarily clings to certain dogmas or doctrines. Some even treat their faith like a hobby, or act like it's a full-time "career." Few are actually being discipled and trained to lay hands on the sick, cast out devils, and win the lost. Few are living the life that is

described in Mark chapter 16.

> *Go ye into all the world, and preach the gospel to every creature. He that believeth and is baptized shall be saved; but he that believeth not shall be damned. And these signs shall follow them that believe; In my name shall they cast out devils; they shall speak with new tongues; They shall take up serpents; and if they drink any deadly thing, it shall not hurt them; they shall lay hands on the sick, and they shall recover.*
>
> (Mark 16:15–18)

Angels and a "Religious" Spirit

If you aren't fervent for the Lord Jesus Christ and or if you are simply going through the motions while "playing church," you may miss your day of visitation or, at the least, you may not recognize it when it comes. You see, Zacharias was a *religious* man. He was always at church. He hung out with the religious crowd at the Temple. But in his private life, he wasn't spiritually "in tune" with God's voice or with God's supernatural ways. Thus, when the angel surprised him with his awesome appearance and his burning message, he was unprepared in his heart and was reticent to believe.

Thus, we see the example of one man who received the ministry of angels, (the prophet Zechariah) and one who did not (Zacharias, the father of John the Baptist)—and we also see the results! We shouldn't be surprised as we begin to see more and more of God's angelic visitations in this end-times reformation.

As for me, I would be very careful not to dismiss all claims of genuine angelic encounters lest the angel of the Lord be displeased, and bring spiritual barrenness and curse upon our lives. Remember, Zacharias was so "busy" serving the Lord and being religious that he didn't have faith to immediately receive angelic instruction. A good way to avoid becoming "spiritually dumb" is to be always open to the supernatural power of God and His angelic activity.

There was another person in the Old Testament who refused the instruction of angels—remember Lot's wife?

Chapter Three

Angels, Humility, and Spiritual Capacity

More often than not, what stops the flow of God's truth regarding the operation of angels (and what prevents us from operating in our supernatural authority in Christ) is quite frankly a lack of humility in our own hearts. All too often the voices of worldliness, the cares of this life, self-ambition, bitterness, unforgiveness, pride, and competition have crowded out His sweet, small voice. If we're going to understand more about God and His heavenly realm, we need humility. It has been said that humility is the "beauty of holiness" and that humility is the glory of the creature because humility empties the soul of pride and self and allows God to be all and all.

What Is Humility?

Humility is teachable. Humility has child-like faith. Humility makes the human heart receptive to the light rays and beams of God's glory and makes it possible for God to willingly share His glory and power with us. Only humility can see God's angels and experience their anointed ministry. Some might think that His glory refers only to His earthly life and ministry, His death and resurrection. But I believe that Jesus is referring to far more than this, for Christ desires His people to get a clearer heaven's-eye view of how beautiful and glorious He truly is.

But only the humble can see His glory. And when believers, by the Spirit and through prayer, see Him in all of His glory, such a revelation will embolden our witness to the world and will make our evangelistic efforts that much more powerful.

And the glory which thou gavest me I have given them;...I in them, and thou in me, that they may be made perfect in one; and that the world may know that thou hast sent me, and hast loved them, as thou hast loved me. Father, I will that they also, whom thou hast given me, be with me where I am; that they may behold my glory, which thou hast given me: for thou lovedst me before the foundation of the world. (John 17:22–24)

Humility is the divine disposition of the heart that allows God to impart Himself into our lives. It gives us the capacity to handle the holy. Humility makes room in the soul of God's servant so God can manifest His power and deliver others through us and do so without such gifts and supernatural manifestations "going to our heads." In fact, humility (and its twin virtue, meekness) is simply knowing that God is all in all and we are nothing without Him and that we are only complete when we abide in Him. Humility is all about our hearts in sync with the meek and lowly heart of Jesus. *It is only through humility that we can be carried to a place where God can trust us with His virtue, truth, and power.* Humility is God's power under control. Walking in pride is both stressful and dangerous, for if God's power were to fall upon a vain and conceited soul, that person's life would explode!

Humility, Mary, and Angels

It's important to know if you're humble. We've all heard the joke that says, "I'm so humble and I'm proud of that!" This isn't the kind of humility I'm talking about. The kind of humility that God looks for is more *God*-conscious than *self*-conscious.

For example, Mary, the mother of Jesus, was chosen for an angelic encounter precisely because of this trait. Because of her humility, God knew that her calling to give birth to the very Son of God would not "go to her head."

*For he has been mindful of the **humble** state of his servant. From now on all generations will call me blessed.*

(Luke 1:48 NIV, emphasis added)

Mary wasn't bragging to her contemporaries or to posterity here. Mary knew she was humble before the Lord and He knew it too. Mary didn't care for the applause of men nor for her social status or even her reputation. Even though she wasn't married, she was willing to admit that she was made pregnant through the power of the Holy Spirit. Remember, in her day and age having a child out of wedlock would have been considered an extremely shameful, rebellious, criminal act. She could not help the fact that God had uniquely chosen her to become impregnated by the Holy Spirit with the very DNA of God. The virgin birth is one of the greatest miracles of the Bible. Of course, the humble always experience miracles and angelic intervention—even if it is at different levels.

Remember the times in which she lived. It would not be good if she appeared to be pregnant with a child if she were not married. In some cases adulteresses were even stoned to death! But because she was humble, she didn't care about public opinion polls. Tabloid-like gossip could not get to her spirit. Since she was dead to self and alive to God, it was no big deal to her if people thought she was ungodly, crazy, or even a harlot! She was willing to suffer for Christ's sake, and the angels were greatly attracted to her. Are you willing to humble yourself and be of no reputation for the cause of Christ? (See Philippians 2:1–12.)

Jesus was kind and humble and endured cruel mocking and slander from unjust sinners. At one point in Jesus' ministry, the jealous religious crowd even went so far as to falsely accuse Jesus of being born of a fornicator. Some liberal, secularist, historical revisionists and DaVinci-ites today are still accusing Him in the same manner!

Then said they to him, We be not born of fornication; we have one Father, even God. (John 8:41)

The envious folks maligned her and her Son, but it didn't matter. She knew her God. She was humble. Mary knew the Lord was her all in all and that apart from Him, her life would be meaningless. She knew she could not give birth to anything without humility.

Her Son Was Her Lord

She was confident in the God of

Abraham, Isaac, and Jacob and did not need the shallow, fleeting praises and recognition that comes from men. This is why she could ponder such an event in her heart and not disclose it to others. *God trusted her.*

Angels, Humility, and Trust

The Lord trusted her with revelation and power from on high. He knew that pride wasn't in her heart, for if it were, the "mission" would have crushed her. Like Abraham before her, she was a humble and true friend of God. She could handle an angelic visitation from the Lord. Mary could also receive angelic help in her life and ministry. Because she was such a friend of God, an angel appeared to her at a crucial point in her life.

I wonder today how many twenty-first-century believers would be sincerely open to receiving such supernatural ministry of angels. Could you handle an angelic visitation from God? I know God judged that in my wife because she pondered the whole thing in her heart for many years and never boasted regarding the experience.

God was well acquainted with Mary's thought and prayer life and knew that she was humbly open to the supernatural realm. So He felt very comfortable sending the angel Gabriel whom He knew she would not refuse. Are you open to God? Are you humbly anticipating a supernatural intervention of God in your life? Jesus said, Blessed are the meek and humble! (See Matthew 5:5.)

Angels—Not to Be Worshipped or Mocked

Paul wrote to the Colossians not to become overly fixated on angels. He also warned them not to worship angels.

> Let no man beguile you of your reward in a voluntary humility and worshipping of angels, intruding into those things which he hath not seen, vainly puffed up by his fleshly mind.   (Colossians 2:18)

But Paul also warned believers not to take for granted the ministry of

authorities—including angels. In other words, we as believers are to have a healthy respect for their ministry in God. This is especially true since they are powerful and righteous creatures.

> Likewise also these filthy dreamers defile the flesh, despise dominion, and speak evil of dignities. (Jude 1:8)

All angels fear God and respect godly authority. They understand delegated authority and are submissive to those who are above them in the Lord. One of the great sins of our carnal age is a lack of respect for all authority.

> But chiefly them that walk after the flesh in the lust of uncleanness, and despise government. Presumptuous are they, self-willed, they are not afraid to speak evil of dignities. Whereas angels, which are greater in power and might, bring not railing accusation against them before the Lord. (2 Peter 2:10–11)

If, then, we are to experience the ministry of angels, it is important that we learn to submit to God and have a healthy fear of the Lord regarding their ministry.

All too many believers today are not capable of giving "birth" to anything that is supernaturally from God. They live in too much pride and skepticism. They lean more to a false sense of security based on their own strength, will power, and self-reliance. We must not trust too much in scientific and empirical observation derived solely from our five physical senses. (See Hebrews 11:1–8.) All the great Bible saints of the past learned to live and walk in the dimension of faith. They learned to exercise the faith that God has given them as a gift.

I'm not suggesting that anyone practice some of the weird New Age techniques regarding angels. No Christian should ever try to call on an angel for help nor should they look to an angel for guidance instead of God. God may send an angel to talk to you or give you guidance, but you shouldn't initiate an encounter. What I'm talking about is practicing the presence of God through the simple application of humble prayer and obedience to God's Word.

A Divine Contrast

Again, *divine expectation and perspective are also vitally important if the Christian is to experience the supernatural ministry of the Holy Spirit and His holy angels.* As I mentioned before, the Bible tells the stories of a priest and a prophet—two Jewish men who had very different perspectives. The *prophet* Zechariah gladly received and embraced the ministry of angels while Zacharias the *priest* did not gladly receive the message and ministry of the angel Gabriel.

Many of us are all too religious and self-reliant like Zacharias. Although many believers mean well, they just don't practice God's presence with humility and pray consistently enough to even attract the possibility that the Lord would visit them in this way. And because of pride, most cannot receive anything from God—let alone from an angel!

The father of John the Baptist, Zacharias, (unlike the prophet Zechariah) was at the opposite end of the spectrum as far as his own pride and unbelief are concerned. As a result, the angel smote him with dumbness.

Let us look again at the text from the gospel of Luke regarding his response.

And the whole multitude of the people were praying without at the time of incense. And there appeared unto him an angel of the Lord standing on the right side of the altar of incense. And when Zacharias saw him, he was troubled, and fear fell upon him....And Zacharias said unto the angel, Whereby shall I know this? For I am an old man, and my wife well stricken in years. And the angel answering said unto him, I am Gabriel, that stand in the presence of God; and am sent to speak unto thee, and to show thee these glad tidings. And, behold, thou shalt be dumb, and not able to speak, until the day that these things shall be performed, because thou believest not my words, which shall be fulfilled in their season.

(Luke 1:10-12, 18-20)

Notice Zacharias' prideful response:

"How shall I know this? For *I...*" This statement is full of ego, self-doubt, fear, and unbelief. James said that a person in such a prideful, unstable state is "double minded" and cannot receive anything from God. Therein is the problem. Rather than saying, "According to Your will be it unto me," Zacharias' response was full of self and unbelief. He couldn't help but look at his natural circumstances and failed to believe the messenger from heaven upon his initial response. This was because his heart wasn't tender and humble before the Lord.

I, Me, My

Since the beginning of time, man has suffered from the sin of pride and self-exaltation. Many professed Christians are infected with an immature spirit that wants to be noticed. They are addicted to a juvenile need of recognition. God's angels do not like pride or juvenile vanity. They should know, for they saw firsthand what evil a self-exalting spirit of pride attempted to perpetrate in heaven.

Through pride, they saw how quickly one-third of their favored angelic friends could fall from the heights. Being overly self-conscious will keep you from experiencing the supernatural realm.

There's a bevy of positive-thinking preachers and false profiteering prophets out there today who are not speaking the whole counsel of God. They withhold truth. They utilize psychology, combined with a gospel that has been "sanitized" with their exclusive positive thinking message.

As a result, the supernatural power and truth of the Scripture has been severely stunted. These sort of folks are always engaging in eccentric histrionics, affectations and slick gospel language to entice their followers with promises without *condition*. There's a plethora of best-selling, positive-thinking, success in life, self-help books out there right now telling you how to "rediscover" yourself and how to fulfill your purpose and destiny. But despite their large congregations and followings, most of it does not reside within

the kingdom of God and is no more than religious hype.

On the other hand, some in the "prophetic" movement now only talk about Jesus as if He were some overly effeminate, pining-away Eros god who is weeping in passionate grief over people who do not want Him but rather love sin. They also solely talk about Him like he was some worldly newlywed lover. They want you to believe that He swoons over you with passionate love as His heart flickers with a longing heartbeat—even while some participate in evil deeds that He is not pleased with! But that's ok, some preach, because you're still trying to "find" yourself in your long journey to acquire some self-esteem. Hell, repentance, sin, the cross, etc., are all but omitted from their contemporary, "prophetic" vocabulary.

What folks really need to do is stop trying to "find themselves" and understand that, when they repent of worldly thinking and meditate upon the Word and obey the Word, they will become God conscious and only then will they find their true fulfillment in Christ. The Lord wants us to "die to the old self" and walk in the newness of His resurrection life. (See Romans 6.) Jesus is our divine master psychologist and knows what's best for each of us.

> He that findeth his life shall lose it; and he that loseth his life for my sake shall find it. (Matthew 10:39 ASV)

In other words, we need to lose more of *our* presence in order to have more of *His* presence. There is nothing like the sweet presence of God to fill the heart and mind. We need less of our presence and more of God's presence. I believe that if John the Baptist's father had esteemed this principle more, he would have avoided some difficulties.

The Perils of Pride

As I've said before, many believers border on becoming "spiritually dumb" because of their latent pride and unbelief in the God of the supernatural. Pride leads to a lack of discernment in the spiritual realm. Pride and unbelief have taken their toll through the ages and have kept multitudes from entering the heavenly regions.

The Fallen Cherub

For example, consider Lucifer's prideful, five "I wills" in Isaiah 14:12–16 and the harmful, devastating effects the spirit of pride and self-exaltation has had throughout the universe ever since. (See Ezekiel 28:11–19.) Pride will always lead to self-reliance, which eventually crumbles. Ambition can be good if one is ambitious *to serve the Lord*. But if one seeks to exalt himself, ambition has devastating effects. One only needs to see the effects of pride on King Nebuchadnezzar.

But when his heart was lifted up, and his mind hardened in pride, he was deposed from his kingly throne, and they took his glory from him: and he was driven from the sons of men; and his heart was made like the beasts, and his dwelling was with the wild asses: they fed him with grass like oxen, and his body was wet with the dew of heaven; till he knew that the most high God ruled in the kingdom of men, and that he appointeth over it whomsoever he will.
(Daniel 5:20–21)

If you want to fall from the heights like Nebuchadnezzar and Lucifer, remain unteachable. Continue to walk in pride. Instead of eating the luscious bread of angels at the King's table, you may end up in the outskirts of heaven eating hay with the oxen!

Self-Titled Egocentrics

Have you been inflicted with a spirit of *self-importance?* Believe me, the Lord and His kingdom will carry on with or without us. We need God more than He needs us. Some folks will try to teach otherwise, but don't listen to them, because they are full of pride, too.

The angels saw what pride did to Lucifer and will not hang out at meetings with a bunch of spiritually self-justifying egocentrics. Sure, there have been a few great Pentecostal leaders of late—men like Derek Prince, Costa Dier, or Brother Andrew, but these kind of saints unfortunately show up on the scene too rarely. Spiritually shallow people today will always claim such spiritual pedigree, but the proof is always in the pudding.

God Has No Grandchildren

Many people today are claiming false legacies. Just because a modern televangelist tells you that they and their cohorts represent the legacy of Azusa Street doesn't make it so. Remember, angels showed up and performed miracles in Jesus' name at Azusa Street mainly because the leaders there were so humble. They were so concerned not to grieve the Holy Spirit's presence (through materialism, covetousness, and pride) that they developed the practice of sticking their heads in apple baskets when they prayed so that no man or woman visiting the meeting would ever think to give them glory! They certainly wouldn't want anyone to "commercialize" their encounter with God under the guise of "celebrating" their revival—(primarily for the purpose of marketing and advertising religious relics and products.) Let's face it: a lot of what's being celebrated is nothing but a ruse for raising money. The real founders of Azusa Street prayed for seven years without any funding or fanfare and they certainly wouldn't want anyone to commemorate their "heart-earned" encounter with God. The holy angels of God are not nearly as close to the modern day marketeers of religious relic and products!

No, my friend, the angels will only feel welcome when the people present are humble and holy. They visited Azusa Street with miracles and signs and wonders mainly because of the humility, intercession, and passion of its leaders. The fact is, leaders in the early charismatic renewal were not overly materialistic nor were they as obsessed with raising money primarily to "make a name for themselves."[1]

In fact, a majority in the full gospel movement today is *not* fulfilling the legacy of either Pentecost or Azusa Street.

Its leadership is full of overly-ambitious, materialistic people who nauseatingly feign a fake religiosity. All too often many of them cannot even be faithful to their own wives or they have fallen victim to greed, lying, deception, arrogance, doctrinal error, pornography, etc.

Yet despite all this they act like they're Spirit-filled but in fact they are simply baptized in a religious spirit. Angels hate religious demons! Christians need to stop giving their time, resources, and money to such vainglory ministries or they will be judged for being a poor steward and for empowering nepotistic celebrities who are basically in the ministry to make money.

Let's be frank—virtually anyone today can self-title themselves "apostle," "reverend," "bishop," "prophet," or "prophetess," etc. Sadly, all too many of these false, self-titled ministers are really spiritual buffoons masquerading as the true. Style is everything to them and if they appear to flourish it is simply because they are good salespeople and put up a good facade. It seems that such preachers are primarily rated by how well they communicate and by how many people view their programming. If their ratings are good, they are seen as a "Christian superstars." And for their live meetings, many times they will carefully select a prominent singer or celebrity to fill in the gaps of their histrionic preaching.

Angels Love Substance—Not Style!

Tragically, such meetings have very little spiritual substance. Very few who attend ever really change. It's basically ninety percent *emotionalism* and ten percent substance. Few leave the meeting absolutely changed to live for Christ. And there will always be little supernatural power present because the angels don't like to hang around Luciferian, egocentric pride-aholics.

Silliness, Seduction, and Scintillation

The prideful are adept at religious manipulation. They are quite experienced with using entertainment and preaching that hypes the people in order to get them to give money. What they cannot achieve through hard-fought prayer and intercession and holy consecrated living, they have supplanted with silliness, seduction, slick manipulation, scintillation, and hucksterism. The saddest thing about all of this is that they actually believe they are serving God and winning souls through their machinations.

Thank God, a move of God is coming where the evil spirit of Egypt, Babylon, and Hollywood—the self-exalting spirit of celebrity, the lust for stardom and worldly fame, the insatiable desire for human applause, the lustful garb and painted faces of Cleopatra and Jezebel—will be banned forever. "Barnum and Bailey" circus-styled Christianity may show you tigers "jumping through hoops" but you will never hear an angel sing or see the power of God!

It's no wonder that so many question the power of God today. It's no wonder that revival tarries. It's no wonder that such silly ideas are now circulating in the body of Christ. Too many Christian leaders have willfully grieved away the presence of the Holy Spirit and God's angels, and have become partakers of evil and worldly compromise. If you want to see an angel, it's important that you ask God to give you pure eyes and pure hearts.

Recovering Prideaholics

Someone with *religious* pride and arrogance will never be able to receive the ministry of angels. If you are struggling with pride and unbelief, that's okay—if you are open to change. God is always eager to visit a life with His Spirit of grace and to forgive us of our sins. Just be honest with the Lord. Humble yourself right now and yield your heart to God like you may have done when you were a little child. Life may have been hard for you and people may have hurt and rejected you. You may have failed Him a million times. Others may mock you and gossip about you. That's okay, too! Jesus knows this and yet He still loves you. He longs to pour His spirit of forgiveness and healing upon you.

The enemy doesn't want you to take down the walls of pride and insecurity that you have built in order to try to protect yourself. The adversary doesn't want God Almighty to visit you in prayer. The enemy doesn't want God and His angels to minister on your behalf. Satan doesn't want you to know the power of God. He doesn't want the Holy Spirit to fill your life so that Christ is formed in you. The enemy doesn't want you to do the works of Christ.

The solution is so simple. If you will sincerely pray to God for help, God *immediately* hears your humble prayer of faith and He sends forth healing, deliverance, prosperity, forgiveness, and redemption to you.

Fallen Kings

The once haughty king of Babylon finally realized that pride and unbelief only led to spiritual blindness and failure.

Now I Nebuchadnezzar praise and extol and honour the King of heaven, all whose works are truth, and his ways judgment: and those that walk in pride he is able to abase. (Daniel 4:37)

Thus, the way up in the kingdom of God is always down. He that is first shall be last. He that is a servant is the greatest of all and *"promotion cometh neither from the east, nor from the west, nor from the south"* (Psalm 75:6), but from God alone.

For God resisteth the proud, and giveth grace to the humble. Humble yourselves therefore under the mighty hand of God, that he may exalt you in due time.
(1 Peter 5:5-6)

If you have lost favor with God through pride, the first step to regaining favor is to simply humble yourself before Him. Then, the Holy Spirit and His angels will draw near to you for they love a broken and contrite heart.

The sacrifices of God are a broken spirit: a broken and a contrite heart, O God, thou wilt not despise. (Psalm 51:17)

For thus saith the high and lofty One that inhabiteth eternity, whose name is Holy; I dwell in the high and holy place, with him also that is of a contrite and humble spirit, to revive the spirit of the humble, and to revive the heart of the contrite ones.

(Isaiah 57:15)

So then, what are the conditions for experiencing angelic ministry? Humility. Humility. Humility. Some of you right now need to get on your knees before God and humble yourselves and pray to your heavenly Father, asking Him for childlike faith. Without a doubt He will answer your prayer and will bless you with His very presence and the presence of His heavenly angels.

Notes

[1] At the turn of the century, a group of Christians experienced the outpouring of the Holy Spirit in what became known as the Azusa Street Revival.

Chapter Four
Angels and Revelation

And I saw another angel fly in the midst of heaven, having the everlasting gospel to preach unto them that dwell on the earth, and to every nation, and kindred, and tongue, and people. (Revelation 14:6)

Angels and Inspiration

Did you know that angels preach the gospel? Many Christians don't realize that a good portion of the law and the Word of God was given to the original inspired writers by angels.

In fact, a good portion of the Word was actually *dictated* directly to the prophets by God's messenger angels.

Those who are skeptical of such angelic encounters quote Scriptures dictated by angels themselves! Without scriptural warrant, you have shrugged off their ministry to the church and have only a "cerebral" understanding of dead orthodoxy

and cold, historic dispensationalism on the matter. You have read too many commentaries written out of the intellect of men. But the Bible is a living, Spirit-inspired book that was given through the Holy Spirit and also with angelic assistance.

Although we are admonished in the Bible not to overly focus on angels or worship them, we should never forget how strategic they have been in giving us the Bible. Throughout church history, we would be remiss not to mention the fact that all great revivals have involved angelic visitations.

At the same time, we also must be careful to check any "message" from an angel to make sure it conforms to the Word of God.

Let no man beguile you of your reward in a voluntary humility and worshipping of angels, intruding into those things, which he hath not see, vainly puffed up by his fleshly mind. (Colossians 2:18)

At the very least, we should all become

more open and aware of their presence. Even though the angelic dispensation of dictation of the written Word of God has closed, we should receive the ministry of angels and the revelation of Jesus they bring in the fear of God and with joy!

Balance Needed

In the past, I liked to think of myself as a seminary-trained, "conservative" Bible student—yet, God has brought so many interesting divine circumstances to me and my family that I had to seriously re-think some of what I was taught earlier in life regarding the dispensation of angels. God sure busted up some of my preconceptions concerning the supernatural realm! Preconceptions can interfere with the Holy Spirit's conceptions and the true revelation that He wants to give.

I firmly believe that the holy, inerrant, infallible, inspired, complete sixty-six canonical books of the Bible are without error, whole and part, and is the final revelation of God. In the book of Revelation, the apostle John warned us not

to add or take away anything from the Word of God. (See Revelation 22:19.) *Yet, this does not mean that we should allow cold, dead orthodoxy, dispensationalism, and traditionalism to cloud over the normal possibility of God's angelic encounters with men and women in this present time.* God never said He would stop visiting His people with visions, dreams, and angelic encounters. Angelic encounters are for the purpose of advancing the plan of redemption and to give direction, encouragement, and protection to His believers and always confirm the Scriptures.

The Angels of Revelation

Like Ezekiel, Daniel, and Zechariah before him, the apostle John experienced the ministry of angels in incomprehensible magnitudes. As a matter of fact, the entire book involves angels from heaven bringing messages on behalf of God's people.

A Biblical View of Angels

Increased Angelic Activity

And when he had considered the thing,

he came to the house of Mary the mother of John, whose surname was Mark; where many were gathered together praying. And as Peter knocked at the door of the gate, a damsel came to hearken, named Rhoda. And when she knew Peter's voice, she opened not the gate for gladness, but ran in, and told how Peter stood before the gate. And they said unto her, Thou art mad. But she constantly affirmed that it was even so. Then said they, It is his angel.

(Acts 12:12–15)

If you have seen an angel or expect angel ministry—do not mind if folks think you are crazy. The early church had a very real and biblical understanding of angels. As we have seen earlier, they even expected them to show up at their prayer meetings! Because the subject of angels is so sensitive to many, I feel compelled to explain the doctrine's firm foundation in Scripture. It's important that we understand the need for holding the Bible in high esteem and adhere to the fact that the Scripture can never be broken.

In Acts 2:14–19 the Bible says that in the last days God will pour out His Spirit on all people who are willing to avail themselves to Him. God will cause those who have sincere faith to have visions and dreams. Signs and wonders will once again become prevalent in the church. In these last days, visions and angelic visitations should not be so surprising to us—as a matter of fact, they will become more prevalent as the coming of Messiah nears.

Historically, we should consider that such supernatural experiences were the foundation upon which the Bible was established and upon which the church stands. In 2 Timothy 3:16, the Bible says, "All Scripture was given by inspiration of God." In Greek, it literally says, "God breathed." The apostle Paul's conversion and subsequent biblical revelations, in which he wrote two-thirds of the New Testament, were all *supernatural in origin.* (See Acts 9:3–12; Galatians 1:11–12; 2:2.) The Bible itself claims it is the Word of God—it is a closed argument.

In a glorious tautology of "circular

reasoning," the Bible claims it is a direct revelation from a supernatural Creator and should not be "tampered" with. In other words, the Bible itself states axiomatically that it is the Word of God. Thus, God has said this in is His eternal Word and the truth of His word and the truth of angels are no longer open for discussion. Period!

Knowing this first, that no prophecy of the scripture is of any private interpretation. For the prophecy came not in old time by the will of man, but holy men of God spake as they were moved by the Holy Ghost.
(2 Peter 1:20)

Verbal and Plenary Inspiration

What Christians need to do is to passionately seek after God in order to know Him and His Word. Some in the New Age movement and even some liberals in the church have gone astray by basing their faith on "experience" rather than on the solid Word of God. Some have gone chasing angels or the miraculous. Others want to have their ears tickled by some new "extra-biblical" revelation that no one else has "tapped into before." They think that no one else in the past two thousand years has heard from God like *they* have. I believe that all sixty-six books of the Bible are infallible. These sixty-six books, and all that is in them (whole and in part), are the fully completed, absolute Word of God.

The whole Bible, Old and New Testament, is a supernatural, direct vision and revelation from God! It is interesting to note that the apostle Paul authored two thirds of the New Testament. And yet, he was quite comfortable with supernatural encounters with God's angels in the work of his ministry.

As we have seen, a good portion of Scripture was actually physically and audibly dictated to the original writers by angels.

And the angel that talked with me came again, and waked me, as a man that is wakened out of his sleep, And said unto me, What seest thou? And I said, I have looked, and behold a candlestick all of gold, with a bowl upon the top of it, and his seven lamps thereon, and seven pipes to the seven lamps, which are upon the top thereof....For who hath despised the day of small things? for they shall rejoice, and shall see the plummet in the hand of Zerubbabel with those seven; they are the eyes of the LORD, which run to and fro through the whole earth.

(Zechariah 4:1-2, 10)

The Revelation of Jesus Christ, which God gave unto him, to show unto his servants things which must shortly come to pass; and he sent and signified it by his angel unto his servant John.

(Revelation 1:1)

And I saw a strong angel proclaiming with a loud voice, who is worthy to open the book, and to loose the seals thereof?

(Revelation 5:2)

In the Old Testament, God revealed His will to men by speaking through prophets. God spoke in direct inspiration through the spirit of the prophet, and the prophet's intellect had no part in the prophe-cy's *origination*. The human imagination was never the source for any revelation of God written in Scripture. In fact, the Lord had spoken by the Holy Spirit to the prophet's spirit first and then the intellect "processed" the inspired word prior to his penning God's words into human language and letters. This is why all the Scriptures, whole and in part, should be considered infallible, inerrant, and without error. God is perfect, and it is God's Word—the Bible claims it, and I believe it! In 1 Thessalonians 5:23, Paul taught us that man is comprised of spirit, soul, and body. God is able through the Holy Spirit to communicate to man's mind through his inner spirit.

Everyday Inspiration

Even though none of us can participate in the divine dictation process as referenced above, all of us can still hear God's voice speak to us specifically through the Word regarding His plans and purposes for our life and ministry. In addition to our private devotions and Bible study,

God will speak to us through the gentle leadings, promptings, and conviction of the still, small voice of the Holy Spirit on a daily basis. This is normally how God speaks to us (sometimes this innate feeling or conviction is often referred to as intuition or a "gut" feeling).

However, there are many instances in the Old and New Testament where the Lord directly spoke to His people with an audible voice and/or with spoken words, or via His angels. In addition, He gave open visions and sent direct messages to His prophets. God spoke to Moses as a man speaks to his friend.

And the LORD spake unto Moses face to face, as a man speaketh unto his friend, and he turned again into the camp.
(Exodus 33:11)

In summary, regarding the Christian doctrine of God, salvation, heaven, hell, and the angels, the sixty-six books of the Bible are a *closed issue* regarding such revelation. No one should ever claim that they have any "new truth" to offer other than what is already in the Bible. When you talk about angels and other such matters, it is easy for one to go overboard with their opinions and thoughts on the matter. However, may we never forget that God can and does still use supernatural gifts and angelic visitations to guide, direct, and help His Christian servants in fulfilling His plans, purposes, and destinies, not only for their lives but for the lives that they will reach for the glory of God.

Counterfeits Presuppose the Real

If there are evil angels, there are also holy angels. If lies presuppose the truth, then counterfeits presuppose the real. All genuine angelic encounters must first be sanctioned by the Lord Jesus Christ! An entire host of cults and heresies have been birthed by "angels of light"—counterfeit angels. Paul warned us to beware lest some angel teach us a different message other than what's in the Bible. The apostle admonished the Galatians in the following passage.

I marvel that ye are so soon removed from him that called you into the grace of Christ unto another gospel: which is not another; but there be some that trouble you, and pervert the gospel of Christ. But though we, or an angel from heaven, preach any other gospel unto you than that which we have preached unto you, let him be accursed.

(Galatians 1:6–8)

Paul plainly spoke of the possibility of evil, fallen angels spreading their Luciferian lukewarm message to believers (normally this is in the form of denying the deity of Christ, the virgin birth, the power of the blood to cleanse from sin, the trinity, and the existence of heaven and hell, etc.). Paul's statement presupposes that if there are *counterfeit* revelations from fallen angels, there are obviously *genuine* encounters. This leaves one to conclude that there should always be the potential (that is, in the normal Christian life) for angelic visitation in the lives of God's people. And, as in the early church, this should be the norm and not the exception.

There is no Scripture that says that at some point in the future (after the New Testament would be canonized) that the angelic encounters or supernatural gifts of the Spirit would cease! What audacity of modern-day Sadducees to attack the supernatural even as they did in Jesus' day—and for the most part, without any scriptural basis. Yes, one day when Jesus returns to set up His heavenly kingdom on earth, the gifts may very well cease but faith, hope, and love shall remain. You need only watch the nightly news to know that we are certainly not in that dispensation yet! (See 1 Corinthians 13:13; 1 John 3:2.)

Angels in Balance

In Colossians 2:18, the apostle Paul also cautioned us not to worship or place heavy focus on angels. But in Hebrews 1:7, 14, the Bible also mentions the vital importance of the ministry of angels in our lives when it says,

And of the angels he saith who maketh his angels spirits, and his ministers a flame of fire....Are they not all ministering spirits, sent forth to minister for them who shall be heirs of salvation?

Paul warned us that Satan can be transformed into an "angel of light." Yet Paul himself received the ministry of holy angels, sent by God, to confirm the gospel he preached. The fact is, most Scripture was supernaturally transmitted revelation from heaven directly to the writer. Paul said of the gospel he preached:

For I neither received it from man, nor was I taught it, but it came through the revelation of Jesus Christ.

(Galatians 1:12 NKJV)

How did Paul therefore get a lot of His revelation? I believe that angels may have even carried Paul into paradise for the purposes of causing him to see the heavenly truths that are now contained in his epistles.

It is not expedient for me doubtless to glory. I will come to visions and revelations of the Lord. I knew a man in Christ above fourteen years ago, (whether in the body, I cannot tell; or whether out of the body, I cannot tell: God knoweth;) such an one caught up to the third heaven. And I knew such a man, (whether in the body, or out of the body, I cannot tell: God knoweth;) how that he was caught up into paradise, and heard unspeakable words, which it is not lawful for a man to utter.

(2 Corinthians 12:1–4)

Although Paul was obviously commanded not to reveal certain revelations concerning heaven and paradise, I'm certain the experience greatly influenced his writings and has given the church much understanding of the heavenly realms. One only needs to read the sixth chapter of 1 Corinthians, the book of Colossians, or the first and second chapters of Ephesians to see that Paul had incredible heavenly perspective truths that could not be discerned through the natural mind.

As a matter of fact, Paul's life on earth was full of examples of angels directing and saving his life in the perils of ministry. Paul knew the reality of these glorious beings firsthand and was not timid to write about these angelic visitations in spite of a very philosophical, intellectual, skeptical, and well-educated, Greco/Roman culture in which he lived.

Regardless, our only true source for sound doctrine and angelology is to be found in the sixty-six books of the Bible.

Have this great assurance and confidence, my friend—angels help you and I to preach the gospel.

Chapter Five
Where Have All the Angels Gone?

Many Christians ask me questions such as, "Why have I never seen an angel?" Or "What does an angel look like?" They should be asking how they should become more *Christlike*. Nonetheless, people are still curious and constantly ask me questions like this. Quite frankly, some of these questions are difficult to answer because it's hard to describe the heavenly in earthly terms.

Someday, you will understand all of this too because you, yourself, will be there in heaven. But one thing is for certain, the angels that visited men and women of God in the Bible were visited primarily because they were godly men and women of prayer.

Daniel was such a prayer warrior. Centuries before Paul's translation into heaven, the young prophet Daniel was having similar encounters of Christ and His angelic hosts.

I saw in the night visions, and, behold, one like the Son of man came with the clouds of heaven, and came to the Ancient of days, and they brought him near before him. And there was given him dominion, and glory, and a kingdom, that all people, nations, and languages, should serve him: his dominion is an everlasting dominion, which shall not pass away, and his kingdom that which shall not be destroyed.
(Daniel 7:13–14)

Many today in the body of Christ are either unknowledgeable or unaware of the angelic hosts that stand ready through the Spirit of God to help them in time of need.

But to which of the angels said he at any time, Sit on my right hand, until I make thine enemies thy footstool? Are they not all ministering spirits, sent forth to minister for them who shall be heirs of salvation? (Hebrews 1:13–14)

You, your family, and your ministry will

have a special place of authority to walk with the angels. You will also have a place where you can stand boldly in Jesus' name and defeat the demonic dark angels as well!

> And the angel of the LORD protested unto Joshua, saying, Thus saith the LORD of hosts; If thou wilt walk in my ways, and if thou wilt keep my charge, then thou shalt also judge my house, and shalt also keep my courts, and I will give thee places to walk among these that stand by.
> (Zechariah 3:6–7, emphasis added)

Spiritual Resistance

Always remember, dear friend, the same angels in the book of Acts that came to the aid of Paul and Barnabas, Peter and others, are still operating on the earth today!

However, a wicked, ingenious, *teeming horde of ancient demonic entities* that opposed those great saints still exist today as well. Because of their several thousand years of scrutiny and observation, they have become supremely adept and very wise concerning human weaknesses. They are always looking for an opening and are on an assignment to destroy every believer on this planet. If they can't destroy you, they will at least attempt to destroy your testimony.

> Be sober, be vigilant; because your adversary the devil, as a roaring lion, walketh about, seeking whom he may devour.
> (1 Peter 5:8)

> I was delivered out of the mouth of the lion. And the Lord shall deliver me from every evil work, and will preserve me unto his heavenly kingdom: to whom be glory for ever and ever. Amen.
> (2 Timothy 4:17–18)

The operation of angels was an indispensable help for the reformation church of this present time. This fact is far underestimated by many Christian leaders today who fail to invoke (in Jesus' name) angelic assistance in their prayers and to take outright authority over evil in their own lives, their families, their churches,

their cities, and their nations. This is a time for *strategic warfare*. Someone who is prayerless and unbelieving, someone who discounts the ministries of holy angels, is easy prey for the enemy. Only the "spiritually violent" will smite the evil principalities of the heavens in this hour.

And from the days of John the Baptist until now the kingdom of heaven suffereth violence, and the violent take it by force.
(Matthew 11:12)

For we wrestle not against flesh and blood, but against principalities, against powers, against the rulers of the darkness of this world, against spiritual wickedness in high places. (Ephesians 6:12)

The authority of the believer and the ministry of angels are powerful revelations in these end times. Understanding the power of the blood of Jesus, the power of the name of Jesus, and your authority as a believer in Jesus Christ will help protect you, your family, your church, and your nation from sickness, disease, poverty, accident, calamity, and even premature death. But there are conditions to their operations. All of God's people should have a healthy fear of the Lord and develop a keener awareness of the spiritual warfare which wages in the heavenlies.

The angel of the LORD encampeth round about them that fear him, and delivereth them. (Psalm 34:7)

For though we walk in the flesh, we do not war after the flesh: (for the weapons of our warfare are not carnal, but mighty through God to the pulling down of strong holds;) casting down imaginations, and every high thing that exalteth itself against the knowledge of God, and bringing into captivity every thought to the obedience of Christ. (2 Corinthians 10:3–5)

Sometimes the only way to defeat evil is through prayer and fasting. (See Matthew 17:21.)

Angels and Worship

In Revelation 8 the Bible describes seven angels with trumpets. (Also see 1 Thessalonians 4:10.) Suffice it to say that angels

88

are fantastic and well-seasoned worshippers. They have been worshipping God since before the dawn of human history.

> Bless the LORD, ye his angels, that excel in strength, that do his commandments, hearkening unto the voice of his word. Bless ye the LORD, all ye his hosts; ye ministers of his, that do his pleasure.
> (Psalm 103:20–21)

> And again, when he bringeth in the first-begotten into the world, he saith, And let all the angels of God worship him.
> (Hebrews 1:6)

Sometimes we need to press in all the more in prayer and fasting to get the results that we are looking for.

The Constancy of Angelic Ministry

It's amazing that most Christians fail to claim the promises of God and invoke the power of the Holy Spirit and angelic hosts on their behalf. (See Hebrews 1:7, 14.) If the early disciples and believers were often protected and directed in their works by angels, why would God change His way of doing things and change His ways of protection now?

Yes, dear saint, Jesus is *"the same yesterday, and to day, and for ever"* (Hebrews 13:8)! Jesus used angels to direct and protect His followers in the early church and He will still do so today. For instance, an angel spoke to Philip directing him to Gaza. (See Acts 8:26.) An angel stood by Paul and talked with him, encouraging and directing him. (See Acts 27:23–24.) An angel, appearing in bright apparel, talked with Cornelius directing him as well to send for Peter. When Peter was in prison an angel rescued him. (See Acts 12:7–8.) These same messenger angels are still available to help God's people in this hour.

The Relevancy of Angels

Where have all the angels gone? In fact, God's angels have not "gone" anywhere. They still come down from heaven into this universe of ours and continue to help establish the church even as they did in the first century. Let's be more open to the "practicalities of their presence." Have you ever danced with angels in your worship? Have you ever felt them safely guide your car around another to avoid an accident?

Who maketh his angels spirits; his ministers a flaming fire. (Psalm 104:4)

All of us need to be more open-minded to their presence. By faith, we must learn to expect more of them than ever in Jesus' name! The kind of angelic visitation that was the norm of the early church should also be the norm today. Angels visited and aided both the apostles and every believer in the early church who were living consecrated, prayerful lives and who were looking upwards.

Are you praying? Are you looking upward? Do you believe in angels and, if you do, do you believe they can bring a miracle from God to your life? The man at the pool of Bethesda believed and even though it took a long while, he finally found his pathway to healing and was not disappointed.

Now there is at Jerusalem by the sheep market a pool, which is called in the Hebrew tongue Bethesda, having five porches. In these lay a great multitude of impotent folk, of blind, halt, withered, waiting for the moving of the water. For an angel went down at a certain season into the pool, and troubled the water: whosoever then first after the troubling of the water stepped in was made whole of whatsoever disease he had....Jesus saith unto him, Rise, take up thy bed, and walk. And immediately the man was made whole, and took up his bed, and walked: and on the same day was the sabbath.

(John 5:2-4, 8-9, emphasis added)

Where have all the angels gone? It's not that they are unavailable to help Christians. I believe the reason contemporary believers do not experience more angelic intervention in their lives is because, unlike the ancients and the early church, few spend the necessary time in earnest prayer patiently waiting upon the Lord for an answer. We've lost some simplicity here. There is a blessed *primitive faith* and patience that the early church possessed that we do not know of.

I believe the solution lies in the believer's continual act of cultivating an earnest prayer life and walking in the presence and the fear of the Lord. It's that simple. For those who do not have a very active prayer life, I suggest starting off with thirty minutes a day, each morning, to earnestly seek the Lord. It isn't about *quantity* of time—it's about the quality of the heart toward God. When you are truly in love with the Lord, three hours alone with Him will seem like thirty minutes!

The Weather Angels

Every moment of the day, the angels of God are intimately involved with your life—this includes even the weather. Did you know that angels are custodians over the elements of nature, including the weather?

And after these things I saw four angels standing on the four corners of the earth, holding the four winds of the earth, that the wind should not blow on the earth, nor on the sea, nor on any tree.

(Revelation 7:1)

And the fourth angel poured out his vial upon the sun; and power was given unto him to scorch men with fire. And men were scorched with great heat, and blasphemed the name of God, which hath power over these plagues: and they repented not to give him glory. (Revelation 16:8–9)

The Purpose of the Song of Angels Project

Whatever your viewpoint is regarding the ministry of angels, the main message of this project is that Jesus Christ loves you and adores you and has commissioned countless angels to help you in your journey to heaven. The angels are also here to assist you in active ministry and warfare if you will only ask the Lord to invoke their help and guidance. When you declare God's Word, Jesus sends them forth. If you humble yourself by faith and ask Jesus to become Lord of your life, I believe God will send His angels into your life immediately and you will feel the very presence of the Holy Spirit. God will move heaven and earth in order to lift you up.

Are they not all ministering spirits, sent forth to minister for them who shall be heirs of salvation? (Hebrews 1:14)

May I repeat, God doesn't want us to focus on angels in an unbalanced manner. But by understanding how they operate, by understanding their service and purpose, we will begin to "see" as Elisha's servant did, that they who are with us are more than they who are against us.

And he answered, Fear not: for they that be with us are more than they that be with them. And Elisha prayed, and said LORD, I pray thee, open his eyes, that he may see. And the LORD opened the eyes of the young man; and he saw: and, behold, the mountain was full of horses and chariots of fire round about Elisha. (2 Kings 6:16–17)

Such a spiritual sight should build up our confidence in God. For when you know that all of heaven is backing you up

with angelic forces, you have no problem speaking the truth in love to anyone.

Open Our Eyes, Lord

Too many have a problem seeing into the spiritual realm. The eyes of many have been made blind and the mouths of many have been made dumb to tell of God's realm of faith. Unlike Zacharias, when God speaks something to us, we need to *immediately* obey.

As an obedient believer, when you become more aware that God and all His angelic hosts of heaven are backing you up, this will certainly give you more confidence in ministering the gospel.

It's my fervent prayer that the Song of Angels project will assist you and help you to see your destiny as a child of God. May God deliver us all from succumbing to "spiritual dumbness." But the Bible says that the spiritually minded are to "judge" (*anikrino*) all things. But we cannot spiritually discern between good and evil in this hour if we don't have spiritual eyes to see and a spiritual tongue to speak forth the word of faith into the heavens.

Conditional Participation

Again, one of the conditional aspects of angel operations is to simply believe that in fact the angels of God have not retreated to another universe but are ready and willing to obey the voice of God in response to our earnest prayer. The very same angels and chariots of fire that encompassed Elisha and his servant are still present with us today. During World War I, a commander called on God for help during a major battle, in which he and his comrades were vastly outnumbered. The angels then appeared in the sky above the enemy and his small troop was able to defeat an entire army!

Where have all the angels gone? They are still present among God's creation and God's people, actively working on behalf of the Father. However, their presence can easily be grieved away through unbelief and habitual sin. This is why it is so important to live holy and to walk in God's grace. Then God may very well open our eyes to see His angelic armies arrayed for battle and ready to fight on behalf of righteousness. God's holy angels are still here with us today ready to take heed to the word of the Lord.

As He did with Elijah's servant, may God Almighty open our eyes to see beyond the veil of this earthly realm!

Chapter Six
Dancing with the Angels

Not only do angels play musical instruments, but they also praise God with their mouths and feet! Many great saints have seen angels dancing before God's throne. In a vision I have seen them even doing cartwheels—not to mention their lofty and dynamic aerobatics! The apostle Paul told the church at Corinth that angels were present at their services. Do you know angels are present in glorious church services? Along with all of God's people, they sing their praises to the Lord in the congregation of the righteous.

Praise ye him, all his angels: praise ye him, all his hosts. (Psalm 148:2)

God's angels also rejoice before Him with exuberant joy! There is a universal way of worshipping God correctly and all creatures who love God rejoice before Him. In the book of Psalms, the Word says that part of this rejoicing includes dancing.

Let them praise his name in the dance: let them sing praises unto him with the timbrel and harp. (Psalm 149:3)

Praise him with the timbrel and dance: praise him with stringed instruments and organs. (Psalm 150:4)

The Bible says all of creation rejoices before God's presence. The Bible says that even God Himself rejoices over us and that there is a time to dance.

The LORD thy God in the midst of thee is mighty; he will save, he will rejoice over thee with joy; he will rest in his love, he will joy over thee with singing. (Zephaniah 3:17)

*A time to weep, and a time to laugh; a time to mourn, and a time to **dance**...* (Ecclesiastes 3:4, emphasis added)

Since the Word also infers that dancing is part of praising the Lord, I believe angels also express their praise through dance. God loves it when we rejoice over Him along with His holy angels, even as He rejoices over us.

Jeremiah prophesied that God's Spirit will raise up a pure, holy chaste virgin (the bride of Christ, which is the church), who will once again rejoice and dance unabashedly and exuberantly before the Lord.

Then shall the virgin rejoice in the dance, both young men and old together: for I will turn their mourning into joy, and will comfort them, and make them rejoice from their sorrow. (Jeremiah 31:13)

There's something very powerful when the people of God joyously dance before the Lord. The joyous stomping of their feet can be felt even in the deepest depths of hell. Now, when I speak of the dance I am speaking about it more in a joyful or Hebrew context rather than some of the more suggestive forms we've seen in the church of late. These suggestive dances have been patterned after the world and not after the tabernacle of David.

David danced mightily before the Lord, as did Miriam and Moses. Dancing before God is an outward expression and natural response of a person in love with his or her Creator. It is also an external symbol of our victory over the evil one and our deliverance from his bondage and tyranny. But the only way we can join in the "dance of the angels" is to be totally surrendered to Christ.

And if we want to dance with the angels, all of us need to plunge ourselves underneath His all-powerful blood.

Without shedding of blood is no remission. (Hebrews 9:22)

Elect according to the foreknowledge of God the Father, through sanctification of the Spirit, unto obedience and sprinkling of the blood of Jesus Christ: Grace unto you, and peace, be multiplied.
(1 Peter 1:2)

We need to consecrate our lives afresh before God this very hour.

I beseech you therefore, brethren, by the mercies of God, that ye present your bodies a living sacrifice, holy, acceptable unto God, which is your reasonable service.

And be not conformed to this world: but be ye transformed by the renewing of your mind, that ye may prove what is that good, and acceptable, and perfect, will of God. (Romans 12:1-2)

A life of true worship means not allowing sin to have dominion over you! A life of true worship means worshippers will yield their lives to the enabling power of the Holy Spirit of grace who works within you the enabling power to do what He's called you to do and to be what He's called you to be in Christ.

For sin shall not have dominion over you: for ye are not under the law, but under grace. (Romans 6:14)

Just think, living a life of holiness means freedom from sin, freedom from depression, freedom from oppression, freedom from a troubled conscience, freedom from inner turmoil, freedom from guilt, freedom from sleeplessness and insomnia—holiness is a great joy to the soul! God wants to make you happy and the angels want you to be happy. But you will never be happy in sin.

In fact, living in a state of holiness is "fun" as well as liberating, because holiness gives you the *capacity* to be used of God. And when you walk with capacity, many wonderful adventures in Christ await you.

The Dawn Treader

Lucifer will always try to "tread" down and oppress the spirit of freedom and liberty in our worship. He hates it when the angels are drawn to our worship. The enemy would like to keep the dawn of Christ's Light from rising in your soul. He would like to tread down the dawn in order to keep your soul in darkness. True prayer and worship will always bring in the presence of God and His angels, and will always cause the Son to rise in our hearts.

Evildoers love darkness. This is why folks with an evil, pharisaical, religious spirit (usually the same people who think they're saved but they're not!) hate it when a brother or sister in Christ affectionately displays their love and passion for the Lord in public. They don't like the Light. It is not simply that they are concerned about things being done *"decently and in order"* (1 Corinthians 14:40). The fact is, they simply don't want anyone dancing or expressing genuine exuberance and joy before the Lord in their praise and worship. They don't like the raising of hands, clapping, and joyous singing in the church. The religious demons in them cannot stand the sounds of glory and joy.

However, some of these churchgoing folks feel quite comfortable drinking a beer while jumping up and down when their favorite football team scores a touchdown. These professed Christians wrongly judge the hearts of others and usually claim that someone is "being out of order" or is trying to "wear religion on their sleeve" or being overly zealous or emotional, etc. It's true that at times someone can draw attention to themselves by acting flaky or disorderly in a church service. But that's not what we're talking about.

Through a self-righteous and mean religious spirit, the devil desires to tread underfoot all expressive praise and worship because it reminds him of what goes on in heaven. When Christians succumb to this oppressive spirit out of the fear of man, this makes God's angels sad because they're always dancing before the Father on the Crystal Sea. Let's face it, the devil doesn't want you or I to dance with joy in the assembly of the saints.

The fear of man bringeth a snare: but whoso putteth his trust in the LORD shall be safe. (Proverbs 29:25)

Pastor, do you want the angels to dance with you and your people in the house of the Lord? Then cleanse your house of demonic strongholds! Learn to exercise dominion over the devil, in Jesus' name! The evil spirit that possessed Michal is still lurking around in the rafters of many of our churches today. And take heed my friend, for there is no one in heaven with an anti-joy, anti-Christ spirit like Michal.

As you might recall, Michal, was the jealous wife of David.

> And *as the ark of the* LORD *came into the city of David, Michal, Saul's daughter looked through a window, and saw king David leaping and dancing before the* LORD; *and she despised him in her heart.*
>
> (2 Samuel 6:16, emphasis added)

Remember, that demon in her knew what it was once like in heaven to dance mightily before the Father. They can no longer join in that dance and they are sick with envy. The evil spirits of hell do not want you to dance for joy before the throne of God.

> *Thou art the anointed cherub that covereth; and I have set thee so: thou wast upon the holy mountain of God; thou hast walked up and down in the midst of the stones of fire. Thou wast perfect in thy ways from the day that thou wast created, till iniquity was found in thee.*
>
> (Ezekiel 28:14–15)

> *And he said unto them, I beheld Satan as lightning fall from heaven.* (Luke 10:18)

Image Breakers

Fallen Lucifer is envious of the power that Christ may delegate to you from on high. In the dawn of man, the evil serpent, the "treader-down," the devil, Satan defiled the pure image of God, the fair vision of Christ. For hasn't the fair image of innocence been restored through the life, death, and resurrection of Jesus Christ? Hasn't He shown us how to walk in His steps and in His image? Didn't the second Adam surpass the first Adam in perfection and holiness? The enemy and many false preachers have defiled the holy image of the Lord through compromised preaching, licentiousness, and failing to give God's precious sheep the full biblical account of how holy, powerful, and pure He truly is. Woe to them!

> *And whosoever shall offend one of these little ones that believe in me, it is better for him that a millstone were hanged about his neck, and he were cast into the sea.*
>
> (Mark 9:42)

But Jesus is calling us to sweet fellowship. For those of you who have despised exuberant worship like Michal; to those of you who have sinned or failed miserably in your life, He is now calling you to Himself and will cleanse you from an evil conscience if you will come to Him.

All of us need to begin to humbly go to Him in prayer and only but seek to rest in His lap like little children. The kingdom of God is for such. And let us look up into the face of our loving heavenly Father like little children—and receive a purer image of who He truly is!

> And said, Verily I say unto you, Except ye be converted, and become as little children, ye shall not enter into the kingdom of heaven. (Matthew 18:3)

> At that time Jesus answered and said, I thank thee, O Father, Lord of heaven and earth, because thou hast hid these things from the wise and prudent, and hast revealed them unto babes. Even so, Father: for so it seemed good in thy sight. (Matthew 11:25-26)

> And he took a child, and set him in the midst of them: and when he had taken him in his arms, he said unto them, Whosoever shall receive one of such children in my name, receiveth me: and whosoever shall receive me, receiveth not me, but him that sent me. (Mark 9:36-37)

Only innocence can dance freely before the Lord with childlike joy.

Only innocence can possess paradise. Only innocence will attract angels. Only with childlike faith that is pure and holy will we see and experience the supernatural power that God longs to manifest in the church in this hour.

Only with humility and total yieldedness to God can we ever expect to hear the angels sing. Only by practicing His Presence and by loving Him supremely out of a pure heart can we experience the supernatural power of God that we have read and heard so much about. It's that simple. Spend more time with God and less with men and you too will hear the angels sing and will be able to dance mightily before the Lord even as God's holy angels are

doing this very moment!

The whole world is waiting. They are hungry to see the true and living God on full display with the love, holiness, power, and truth of God radiating from your life.

Foot Shackles

Sadly, there are no longer many angels dancing at some religious services these days. This is because some religious folks have shackled the church services by not creating a godly and holy atmosphere for them to enter into worshipping with the people present. Some churches have even banned Christians from dancing during the praise and worship time. They have a Michal spirit—they would deny the Miriams and Davids from exalting the Lord in the dance.

Because of moral mixture in the camp, angels don't feel welcome in many services today. As we have seen above, angels are repulsed when Christians fear man rather than God. They are repulsed when a soul commits willful habitual sin and lives in a spirit of unforgiveness, bitterness, unbelief, murmuring, complaining, anger, compromise, lust, gossip, etc. But God's angels always have a "free hand" to work on your behalf even as they were able to freely work on behalf of the prophet Daniel.

We have seen the effects of purity and innocence in the life of Daniel. Daniel trusted God completely—no matter what circumstance he was in. It didn't matter if he was in the king's courts or the lion's den. He was a pure worshipper. The angels are also pure worshippers and are strongly drawn to holy and pure worship. Like God, they also love purity and innocence even as they are innocent and pure. Spiritually, like attracts like. For innocence is unimpaired integrity. The Bible doesn't say whether Daniel danced before the Lord, but I'm certain that he did. No one could have that great of ministry without living in a life of joyful worship.

Handcuffed!

Willful and habitual sin and iniquity, deceit, crookedness, perverseness, moral distortion, and the bending and perverting of God's moral laws mean a person is no longer innocent and therefore, it is impossible for them to partake of liberating worship unless they humble themselves and repent before a loving God who is willing to restore them on the spot.

If my people, which are called by my name, shall humble themselves, and pray, and seek my face, and turn from their wicked ways; then will I hear from heaven, and will forgive their sin. (2 Chronicles 7:14)

It is impossible to joyously dance before the Lord with a heart full of vice. When a person is not dwelling in a state of innocence, the promises of God seem unattainable because evil thought patterns and wicked imaginations of unbelief have clouded their eyes to God's miracle-working power. *The angels are handcuffed!* They are not able to work on their behalf and there is no shelter or sure protection from evil.

But through childlike faith in the Word and by walking in humility and purity before God, the Lord has given us the keys to unlock angelic intervention in our generation. You too can dance with the angels.

Let us therefore come boldly unto the throne of grace that we may obtain mercy, and find grace to help in time of need.

(Hebrews 4:16)

Chapter Seven
Angel Facts

A Little Lower Than the Angels

Initially, God created Adam and Eve just a *"little lower than the angels."*

> Thou madest him a little lower than the angels; thou crownedst him with glory and honour, and didst set him over the works of thy hands. (Hebrews 2:7)

It's true that a born-again believer even now has more authority and power in Jesus' name than the angels—but this is only in a legal and positional sense. For no man or woman can travel at the speed of light or destroy 185,000 Assyrians in one day! No human being can pivot from one dimension to the next at will. No man, woman, or child can walk through the wall of a home or ascend up into heaven with incomprehensible speed and velocity. But one warrior angel can do all these. However, the Christian will receive a body of light that will have greater powers than even the angels.

The Strange Fire of Lucifer

After original sin and a steep fall from grace, Adam and Eve became virtually emptied of all truth. They became "sin-marred," distant images of God. Adam and Eve's glorious eternal bodies of light became darkened, carnal flesh. Through sin and the ambitious fire of Lucifer, the laws of physics had been disrupted and had come under the bondage of the fallen laws of nature. Scientists and astrophysicists tell us today that natural laws of the universe, such as the law of entropy (the limitation on the amount of energy that can be used in a closed, living eco-system), the law of gravity and general relativity, and the first and second laws of thermodynamics, all tend to restrict not only our life span but our ability to travel effortlessly throughout the universe, etc. It's true that God created the natural laws of the universe but not in their current formula. There's too much death and destruction in the universe. There are too many accidents and senseless tribulations and calamities.

All of us now know that since the fall, unredeemed mankind is destined to hard work, labor, pain, and suffering in this life. Sin has vitiated the original plan of God for man. Instead of basking in the light rays of God's glory in a garden protected from cosmic rays and the negative effects of interstellar space—they were thrown in the midst of the intergalactic battle of the good forces of Michael versus the evil forces of Lucifer. Instead of living in great wealth, abundance, and incredible prosperity; instead of walking in a body that would never grow old; instead of living in peaceful purity and innocence before God, they had now become personally wise unto evil.

Adam and Eve (and all of God's people ever since) have been infected with original sin. The strange and ambitious fire of Lucifer had spread like a vicious conflagration through each and every heart of the sons of Adam. There has been war and rumor of war ever since. There has been crime, accident, calamity, and sorrow ever since. Even now this sin principle works within every person on the earth and can only be conquered through the blood of Jesus, the Word of God, and the grace of God.

Yet, through Christ's victory on Calvary, all of the disrupted and defiled natural world and all the disrupted and defiled spiritual world have now legally been healed in Christ. In other words, the natural world and the spiritual world has become one and perfected in Christ. However, the final manifestation of this in both realms awaits the day of the restitution of all things.

Whom the heaven must receive until the times of restitution of all things, which God hath spoken by the mouth of all his holy prophets since the world began.

(Acts 3:21)

Even still, both the natural world and the spiritual world have been made one in Christ and have now been reconciled to the Father through the Son. The holy, sweet, and pure fire of Christ has now consumed the false fire of Lucifer.

The Merciful Cherubim of Eden

The tree of life is an actual tree. God is not speaking figuratively here. There would have been big trouble if Adam and Eve had eaten of it after they had eaten of the tree of the knowledge of good and evil.

Now the serpent was more subtle than any beast of the field which the Lord God had made. And he said unto the woman, Yea, hath God said, Ye shall not eat of every tree of the garden? And the woman said unto the serpent, We may eat of the fruit of the trees of the garden: but of the fruit of the tree which is in the midst of the garden, God hath said, Ye shall not eat of it, neither shall ye touch it, lest ye die. And the serpent said unto the woman, Ye shall not surely die: for God doth know that in the day ye eat thereof, then your eyes shall be opened, and ye shall be as gods, knowing good and evil. And when the woman saw that the tree was good for food, and that it was pleasant to the eyes, and a tree to be desired to make one wise, she took of the fruit thereof, and did eat, and gave also unto her husband with her; and he did eat. And the eyes of them both were opened, and they knew that they were naked; and they sewed fig leaves together, and made themselves aprons....so he drove out the man; and he placed at the east of the garden of Eden Cherubims, and a flaming sword which turned every way, to keep the way of the tree of life.

(Genesis 3:1–7, 24)

Many think physical death was too severe a judgment on Adam and Eve, but God allowed it in order to prevent eternal spiritual death. God gave them both free will. He did not create robots. He did not desire to operate a "wooden man" on a string like some ventriloquist. God would not be pleased to move a battery-operated humanoid, like some toy. Nor did He desire to animate man like a remote-controlled automobile. God gave every man, woman, and child a free will. Mankind is free to imagine, think, choose, and create.

Because Adam and Eve had willfully allied with Satan and chose to *personally experience evil*, God was merciful and didn't want them to be eternally frozen in such a sinfully moral state. He did not want to "immortalize" their sin nature. He did not want the "sin life" to become their eternity life. Therefore, through merciful Cherubim, with flaming swords, He forever banned them from the garden of Eden.

The fact is, our physical and spiritual first parents had already eaten from the tree of the knowledge of good and evil and if they had then eaten from the tree of eternal life, all of mankind ever since may have been locked into a wicked spiritual state forever! Always remember dear saint, it was merciful angels that under God's direction, protected mankind from spiritual and eternal death. And by the way, don't worry—the tree of life has been taken to heaven where it has been safely "transplanted" along the avenue heading to the throne of God.

Then the angel showed me the river of the water of life, bright as crystal, flowing from the throne of God and of the Lamb through the middle of the street of the city. On either side of the river is the tree of life with its twelve kinds of fruit, producing its fruit each month; and the leaves of the tree are for the healing of the nations.
(Revelation 22:1–2 NRSV)

Again, to accomplish this, God mercifully placed a cherubim with a flaming sword who would prevent them from ever re-entering paradise until the Son of Man would totally recreate and restore the new garden of Eden. In the garden of paradise, the tree of life is now in full bloom and the redeemed will freely partake of its delicious, life-giving fruit forever.

Until then, the human race has been and will be continually bombarded by the effects of original sin. We see tragedy, violence, terror, and hardship every day across this planet. And don't continue to torment yourself by asking the same question over and over again: "Why does God allow for evil and tragedy?" After all, God could have wiped out the entire human race in Genesis chapter six, but He decided that there was great potential for mankind through His Son Jesus Christ.

Yes, the effects of original sin have wreaked havoc on the entire universe. Daily we see such harmful effects on the human body. And no nutritionist, plastic surgeon, or cosmetologist can stop it, even though they may graciously delay it for a short time! After all, Paul did say that nutrition and exercise had yielded some profit. But compared to God working within us righteousness and the eternal weight of glory it should be low on the list of spiritual priorities. So rejoice and get the heavenly perspective.

For which cause we faint not; but though our outward man perish, yet the inward man is renewed day by day.

(2 Corinthians 4:16)

We're all getting old, but that's okay. We have nothing to fear from old age and death. Paul had been caught up into heaven itself. He had been translated by God to that new Eden in paradise. Thus, he could say this about life on earth:

For our light affliction, which is but for a moment, worketh for us a far more exceeding and eternal weight of glory; While we look not at the things which are seen, but at the things which are not seen: for the things which are seen are temporal; but the things which are not seen are eternal.

(2 Corinthians 4:17–18)

For to me to live is Christ, and to die is gain. But if I live in the flesh, this is the fruit of my labour: yet what I shall choose I wot not. For I am in a strait betwixt two, having a desire to depart, and to be with Christ; which is far better: nevertheless to abide in the flesh is more needful for you.

(Philippians 1:21–24)

Remember, even after the fall, all was not lost for there was a faithful majority of holy and obedient angels. As a matter of fact, two-thirds of the angels remained faithful to God and, along with Michael, fought evil on God's behalf. To this day, these angels are full of God's light, protect paradise, help us in our journey to heaven, and instantly perform God's word at His command. As they were in Eden, they are still merciful creatures!

Angels and Prayer

No believer should ever presume that they have some hidden "New Age power" in commanding or decreeing God's angels to do things for them or for others. In Psalm 103:20, the Bible says that *angels only operate as the Word of God is declared by the Lord's saints.*

> *Bless the Lord, ye his angels, that excel in strength, that do his commandments, hearkening unto the voice of his word.*
> (Psalm 103:20)

As intercessors in the body of Christ, we need, like the prophet Daniel, to fast, pray, and war against the evil principalities that reign over our cities and nations. We must begin to surrender to God and bind the strongman and take authority over his dominion with humility, brokenness, and repentance. As we seek God, then God will rebuke the devourer and ruling demonic powers over the geographical area we are interceding for. Do you want revival in your city or town? Let us therefore understand the ministry of angels and the importance of praying them into action by the authority in the Word of God and the name of Jesus!

The prophet Daniel described the awesome appearance of an archangel in the following passages that show the archangel would eventually smite the demon of Persia on his behalf:

> *Then I lifted up mine eyes, and looked, and behold a certain man clothed in linen, whose loins were girded with fine gold of Uphaz: his body also was like the beryl, and his face as the appearance of lightning, and his eyes as lamps of fire, and his arms and his feet like in colour to polished brass, and the voice of his words like the voice of a multitude....Then said he unto me, Fear not, Daniel: for from the first day that thou didst set thine heart to understand,*

and to chasten thyself before thy God, thy words were heard, and I am come for thy words. But the prince of the kingdom of Persia withstood me one and twenty days; but lo, Michael, one of the chief princes, came to help me; and I remained with the kings of Persia....Then there came again and touched me one like the appearance of a man, and he strengthened me....Then said he, Knowest thou wherefore I come unto thee? and now will I return to fight with the prince of Persia: and when I am gone forth, lo, the prince of Grecia shall come. But I will show thee that which is noted in the Scripture of truth: and there is none that holdeth with me in these things, but Michael your prince.

(Daniel 10:5-6, 12-13, 18, 20-21)

God wants to evict every demonic presence reigning over every home, village, city, and nation on this planet! Through the name of Jesus and through the blood of Jesus, His church has been thoroughly empowered to accomplish this.

And I say also unto thee, That thou art Peter, and upon this rock I will build my church; and the gates of hell shall not prevail against it. (Matthew 16:18)

As believers, the choice is ours. In fact, all progress and any spiritual success we ever have in this life must be considered prayer successes. Conversely, any failures we experience as a believer are, quite frankly, prayer failures. The angels await your intercessions in order for God to mobilize them.

The Ancients' Advantage

Fewer distractions! I believe the ancients spent far more time seeking the face of God than we do today, which is one reason why they encountered angels so often. To them, this seemed to be a "normal" occurrence in their spiritual life. Could it be that God is trying to reawaken in some of us that keen spiritual thirst for prayerful relationship and meditation on the deep things of God and the Spirit? Once again, the whole world will be turned upside-down by Christians who have been connected to heaven's throne through the power of prayerful contemplation of the Word and of an abiding relationship with Christ.

Abraham's Angels

The patriarch, Abraham, was very familiar with angelic ministry and welcomed God's servants into his life and ministry. One time, he even invited the pre-incarnate Christ and His angelic entourage to have dinner with him!

> And he lift up his eyes and looked, and, lo, three men stood by him: and when he saw them, he ran to meet them from the tent door, and bowed himself toward the ground,...and I will fetch a morsel of bread, and comfort ye your hearts; after that ye shall pass on: for therefore are ye come to your servant. And they said, So do, as thou hast said. And Abraham hastened into the tent unto Sarah, and said, Make ready quickly three measures of fine meal, knead it, and make cakes upon the hearth. And Abraham ran unto the herd, and fetcht a calf tender and good, and gave it unto a young man; and he hasted to dress it. And he took butter, and milk, and the calf which he had dressed, and set it before them; and he stood by them under the tree, and they did eat.

(Genesis 18:2, 5–8)

From this passage, we see that angels can eat food if they like. And for you folks who like to eat on earth, don't be concerned, there are banquet halls throughout heaven where a "heavenly church picnic" is always prepared for you!

Angels, Intercession, and Strategic Warfare

Let's consider the power of intercession in the life of Abraham. In one sense, we live in a world very similar to Abraham's. Sexual perversion, homosexuality, immorality, and a love of violence has gripped our entire culture. We live in a Sodom and Gomorrah-like culture. For the most part, it appears that the modern-day church has lost the "culture war." The ordaining and marrying of homosexuals is but a final indicator of the judgment and wrath that will come. The mocking of God's order of procreation and morality will no longer be tolerated.

Jesus, the Son of God (and also the greatest of all the prophets), correctly predicted that the last generation would be as "in the days of Noah." One famous evangelist's wife has stated that if God doesn't judge America, He owes Sodom and Gomorrah an apology!

But there is always hope if Christians will begin to pray in earnest! In Genesis 18:23, the angels could not destroy all the towns in the region of Sodom and Gomorrah at that time because of Abraham's intercessions! You see, Abraham had relatives in that town.

And the men turned their faces from thence, and went toward Sodom: but Abraham stood yet before the Lord. And Abraham drew near, and said, Wilt thou also destroy the righteous with the wicked?...And he spake unto him yet again, and said, Peradventure there shall be forty found there. And he said, I will not do it for forty's sake. (Genesis 18:22-23, 29)

And it came to pass, when they had brought them forth abroad, that he said, Escape for thy life; look not behind thee, neither stay thou in all the plain; escape to the mountain, lest thou be consume.... And Abraham gat up early in the morning to the place where he stood before the Lord: and he looked toward Sodom and Gomorrah, and toward all the land of the plain, and beheld, and, lo, the smoke of the country went up as the smoke of a furnace. And it came to pass, when God destroyed the cities of the plain, that God remembered Abraham, and sent Lot out of the midst of the overthrow, when he overthrew the cities in the which Lot dwelt. (Genesis 19:17, 27-29)

In Genesis 19:22-29, God remembered Lot because of Abraham's prayers and the angels spared Lot's life while destroying Sodom and Gomorrah. The question is, are there enough interceding, righteous souls today to spare the far greater number of the wicked from a thermonuclear blast of God's judgment—a judgment for the great sins of our land—sins such as abortion, the mass exportation of

violence, pornography, filth, and occult. A judgment because the high priest has abandoned his position in the home and has failed to love his wife and raise his children in the Scriptures and in prayer. I pray we would begin to intercede for this nation with importunity and a sense of divine urgency.

The Early Church and Angels

In Acts 12:1-1, Peter's life was spared through intercession and the ministry of angels. We need to begin to pray the angels into action and understand their role in end-times revival. In Acts 10:3, Peter was given clear vision and direction by an angel of God. In Acts 27:23, Paul said no harm would come to those on a ship he was on because the angel of the Lord was with them. There are many more examples of angelic intercession too numerous to mention here.

The angels wait for God's orders to come in answer to our prayers, even as they stand on the brink to invade the dark principalities that control a generation that walks in darkness. Millions of them remain sidelined. Again, all of us need to break before God in repentance and humility and pray for those professed Christians around us who "talk the talk" but are not walking morally right before God. We need to have enough love to stand in the gap and pray for true and sure conversion for their eternally endangered souls.

And I sought for a man among them, that should make up the hedge, and stand in the gap before me for the land, that I should not destroy it: but I found none.

(Ezekiel 22:30)

Angels on the Northern Plane

Heaven and the angels' abode exist on a higher realm of reality and in another dimension far greater than this one. Angels are able to come into our plane or sphere of existence and they are also able to re-ascend to their higher realm of existence—their own "northern plane." In a vision, I saw that when a child of faith dies, they are set free from their bodily encumbrance and an angel takes them northward by the hand and ascends into heaven with them. The dark principalities of evil hosts in the mid-heavens will attempt to hinder the passage of the angel and the saved soul. But their charges, curses, accusations, blasphemies, and resistance are easily overcome by the angel's trust in Christ, and by his powerful praise. And when the ascent consummates at the very gates of glory, the soul will continue its ascent toward the north where the throne of God is positioned.

Each soul will be welcomed at the gate with singing, dancing, and rejoicing to a royal welcome beyond our wildest imagination. One day, all of us will feast with Jesus, Abraham, Isaac, and Jacob. We, too, will join with the saints and the angels in the wedding supper of the Lamb, celebrating a victorious homecoming within this glorious plane of existence—even within the northern plane of God! And never forget, precious saint, this is the highest form of existence and life conceivable—or inconceivable for that matter!

The Voice of an Angel?

Anyone who ever claims that he or she has the "voice of an angel" surely must be speaking *figuratively*. If they're not, then it's most likely that they have never heard an angel sing! Of course, you could say that he or she tries to sing like an angel or that their voice is angelic. But the anointed sweetness and power of angelic voices, their incredible dynamic range, the euphonic timbre and love and purity in which they sing to the glory of God has no rival on earth!

Angels sing with perfect voice and with a perfect heart—free and innocent of any motives, vanity, self-exaltation, pride, or lust. No seductive, clingy, dirty garments for them. No wretched "look at me" choreography with lusty body movements. No group dancing that distracts the audience from focusing on Christ or that turns the congregation into "seat warming" spectators. No filthy hip shaking and pre-planned stage moves. No "stage presence," but His Presence! No worldly Broadway act needs to be imported into the church in order to reach others for Christ.

The angels love the preaching of the true Word of God. They love to enforce God's commandments and to reveal the supernatural power of God. They confirm God's Word.

Bless the Lord, ye his angels, that excel in strength, that do his commandments, hearkening unto the voice of his word.
(Psalm 103:20)

Faith honors God, and God honors faith. Just because certain theologians and church leaders think the topic of angels to be foolish doesn't mean that it is.

Because the foolishness of God is wiser than men; and the weakness of God is stronger than men.
(1 Corinthians 1:25)

And they went forth, and preached everywhere, the Lord working with them, and confirming the word with signs following. Amen. (Mark 16:20)

For the kingdom of God is not in word,

but in power. (1 Corinthians 4:20)

No person should think that they can conjure up or decree with their own will the ministry of angels. All the power of God is from the Lord.

But we have this treasure in earthen vessels, that the excellency of the power may be of God, and not of us.
(2 Corinthians 4:7)

Why Most Christians Never Hear Angels Sing

Certain backslidden church leadership feels the need to turn the church into a "theater" because, quite frankly, there is not enough primitive power and fire in their preaching. Their rationale for copying the world and its modes of entertainment are inane. They think they are becoming "seeker friendly" and "cultural bridges," but the power of the gospel will not be mixed with strange fire.

Believe me, when the world sees the true power of God resident in the church, these preachers will not find the need to

go down to Egypt for their evangelism techniques. Truly, at best these types of egocentric leaders are boring. The angels refuse to attend their meetings. They constantly grieve the Holy Spirit, and like shallow "talk show hosts," they trade the power of God for man's wit and shallow thinking.

Chapter Eight
How to See an Angel

Recently, I heard a brother give a fascinating account regarding a pastor friend of his. The pastor shepherded a very large and successful church, yet he knew that God had something more in store for his life. He was also concerned about the absence of God's supernatural presence in his own life and ministry. This pastor had a very precious young boy who was about six years old. The boy was a very obedient child and very pure and innocent concerning evil. (See Daniel 6:20–22.) This young child loved to sing praise songs and prayed continually to the Lord in his bedroom.

At some point in time, he began to have visitations from an angel, because his dad could see him talking to another person in the room even though no one else was there. At first the father thought the boy was talking to himself, but he later realized he was talking to an unseen angelic friend. It was interesting to the father that the boy was so peaceful in his disposition as he spoke with this angel. One day, the boy's father asked the boy who he was talking to. The boy said, "I am talking to my angel friend."

The boy's father then said, "Son, please ask the angel why I cannot see him also?"

His young son then posed this question to the angel. After the angel spoke, he turned to his father and said...

"The angel told me the reason you do not have eyes to see him is because your own eyes have beheld too much evil and your spirit has become far too callous."

In tears, the father then asked, "Please ask him if I will ever be able to see him."

On behalf of his father, the boy then asked the angel this question and when the angel replied, the boy smiled and said.

"Yes, one day you will be able to see him too, but he said it will take a long time to wear the calluses off your soul so that you will be able to converse with him too."

Innocence and the Ministry of Angels

If we are to see into the glory realm where the angels abide, like Daniel, we must pray for the power of innocence to be working in our lives.

Today, too many hearts have become hardened by sin and by the propensity to look upon evil. This was also true for the culture in which Daniel was raised as a young boy. What made Daniel different was that he refused to look upon the evils of the society of that era. He refused to *imbibe* of sin and shunned peer pressure in order to walk purely before the Lord. This is one of the reasons why his friends, Shadrach, Meshach, and Abednego were able to see the fourth man with them in the fiery furnace—because purity and innocence was found in them by God.

He answered and said, Lo, I see four men loose, walking in the midst of the fire, and they have no hurt; and the form of the fourth is like the Son of God.

(Daniel 3:25)

Later in his life, the attribute of humility and purity in Daniel's life led to another angelic encounter and miracle. After being thrown into a lion's den by a rebellious king, the angels worked on behalf of Daniel, shutting all their angry, ravenous, man-eating mouths, preventing them from having a morning meal. God was able to shut the mouths of lions because a childlike innocence of evil was found to be resident in Daniel's heart—even as a young adult.

And when he came to the den, he cried with a lamentable voice unto Daniel: and the king spake and said to Daniel, O Daniel, servant of the living God, is thy God, whom thou servest continually, able to deliver thee from the lions? Then said Daniel unto the king, O king, live for ever. My God hath sent his angel, and hath shut the lions' mouths, that they have not hurt me: forasmuch as before him innocency was found in me; and also before thee, O king, have I done no hurt.

(Daniel 6:20–22, emphasis added)

There is real power in living in moral

purity. There is power in *innocence*. There is real power in godly character and integrity. If you want to walk with angels like Zechariah and administer the gospel of Jesus Christ with real power in this last hour, it's vitally important that you surrender your entire heart to Christ without delay and ask Him to purify your garments. Garments always represent your moral character and ministry. And the blood of Jesus will wash whatever sins you have committed if you will but ask Him to cleanse you of them.

If you have failed in the past, the Lord will help you. Through His grace, God will restore you if you are willing to surrender to Him. Even now, if you will but ask, Jesus will fully restore innocence and transparency in your heart and life in an instant. It's your choice—you can either continue to watch evil on television and in movies, imbibing of the ungodly, idolatrous, occult spirit of violence that this world has to offer, and never see an angel and never touch the heavenly realm. Or you can humble yourself and yield your will to God's enabling grace in order to follow God with a pure heart. Purity is an important thing to the Father. Jesus said, only "the pure in heart will see God..."

Blessed are the pure in heart: for they shall see God. (Matthew 5:8)

For without holiness no man will see the Lord.

Follow peace with all men, and holiness, without which no man shall see the Lord. (Hebrews 12:14)

Flee also youthful lusts: but follow righteousness, faith, charity, peace, with them that call on the Lord out of a pure heart. (2 Timothy 2:22)

Let no man despise thy youth; but be thou an example of the believers, in word, in conversation, in charity, in spirit, in faith, in purity. (1 Timothy 4:12)

The elder women as mothers; the younger as sisters, with all purity. (1 Timothy 5:2)

Regardless of peer pressure or modern arguments against legalism and holiness,

God is still searching for hearts that are humble and pure so He can supernaturally move through them to touch a lost and dying world for the glory of Christ. There are a lot of big ministries out there that appear to be having a major impact. Unfortunately, a lot of it is nothing but slick marketing, brand-name advertising, "professional" presentation, histrionics, and a lot of hype.

There is a lot of ranting and railing about this and that, a lot of quips and quotes, and clever and witty sermons—yet, all with very little spiritual substance and content. This is because the leaders of these ministries have become jaded with a lust for ambition, materialism, and a love of notoriety. As a result, there is very little real discipleship and Christlikeness being built into their followers. Some have called this twenty-first-century phenomenon a glitzy form of TV/entertainment Christianity. As recent statistical studies show, all the major sins and the crimes that they represent are sky-rocketing.

Many church members have stumbled because they have been reduced to mere spectators. The early church was not so. All the people of God were actively involved in teaching and evangelism or some sort of helps ministry. Many have fallen prey to sedentary Christianity and by surfing the channels too much have become jaded and polluted by the wicked imagery through television. Angelic activity has been restrained to say the least.

Grace That Is Greater

God's grace and mercy is abundant. God is a good God and a forgiving God. He loves you infinitely and will always provide ample time for you to come to Him. No one should feel condemnation because they have not arrived. If the Lord has chastened you, it's only for your liberty. God doesn't want you to be overly concerned for He is calling you so that you may repent so He can restore and heal you. And if through sin, you have somehow lost the innocence and purity you once enjoyed, God will be loving and merciful to you.

Many long to regain the "carefree," happy, childlike heart and pure conscience they enjoyed many years ago. One thing for sure, in heaven all of us will be restored fully to childlike innocence and purity. Maybe some circumstance or even some person has robbed you of that in the past. But to those who yield to God today, this state of transparency and innocence is attainable even at this very moment.

Yes, the world and people can be mean. But we need to forgive and release others. The devil is treacherous and cruel and has scarred and maimed the image of God in many a precious soul. But Jesus is the great restorer. God is so merciful. Therefore, humble yourself, repent for the foolishness of your sin and the blood of Jesus will cleanse you from every sin and erase all your bad memories.

As far as the east is from the west, so far hath he removed our transgressions from us. Like as a father pitieth his children, so the LORD pitieth them that fear him. For he knoweth our frame; he remembereth that we are dust. (Psalm 103:12–14)

Come now, and let us reason together, saith the LORD: though your sins be as scarlet, they shall be as white as snow; though they be red like crimson, they shall be as wool. (Isaiah 1:18)

And they shall teach no more every man his neighbour, and every man his brother, saying, Know the LORD: for they shall all know me, from the least of them unto the greatest of them, saith the LORD: for I will forgive their iniquity, and I will remember their sin no more. (Jeremiah 31:34)

He will turn again, he will have compassion upon us; he will subdue our iniquities; and thou wilt cast all their sins into the depths of the sea. (Micah 7:19)

If we confess our sins, he is faithful and just to forgive us our sins, and to cleanse us from all unrighteousness. (1 John 1:9)

God will totally forgive and restore you to primitive, virginal, Edenic purity and joy—now that's grace!

PART II
THE MUSIC

"The Song of Michael"

A Return to Primitive Worship Forms

The early church walked in great supernatural power, love, and holiness. Some of the things they did were to gather together on a daily basis for the purpose of prayer and the daily breaking of bread. They walked in power evangelism and transformed the cultures in which they lived. (See Acts 2:1.) Several of the songs have lyrics that are based upon the early church hymns that were sung in the language of its day—namely Roman Latin. Some of the music below such as *"Adoramus," "Ave Verum,"* and "Stay with Me" contain actual words from ancient early church liturgies and manuscripts and are also sung in Latin. The simplicity of their art form and their open love for the holiness of God is evident throughout the lyrics.

Make no mistake about it—prayer, fasting, practicing the Lord's Supper, and walking in humility and holiness attracts the presence and power of God. And whenever God is present, the supernatural power of God will manifest and souls will be converted into the kingdom of our Lord and Savior Jesus Christ.

An Identifyable Flying Object

When Michael flies down into earth's atmosphere to herald the Lord's return, he will be easy for all to identify!

We hope and pray these songs will inspire you to look up to the right hand of the throne where Jesus is seated. The day of the Lord is upon us and Michael is about to make a stellar announcement.

> *For the Lord Himself shall descend from heaven with a shout, with the voice of the archangel, and with the trump of God: and the dead in Christ shall rise first.*
>
> (1 Thessalonians 4:16)

The Song of Michael

> *And at that time shall Michael stand up, the great prince which standeth for the children of thy people: and there shall be a time of trouble, such as never was since*

there was a nation even to that same time: and at that time thy people shall be delivered, every one that shall be found written in the book. And many of them that sleep in the dust of the earth shall awake, some to everlasting life, and some to shame and everlasting contempt. (Daniel 12:1–2)

The song of Michael will close this current church age. God takes pleasure in delegating authority to godly saints and angels of all ranks. In this case, Michael is the one He has delegated to announce the end of this *aeon* (i.e., age). Although the Song of Angels is a song solely sung to the glory of Jesus (for He is the Song of Songs!), there is a special song of decrees that Michael will sing that is both earthward and hell-ward. It is a song of great power and authority over all the evil forces of the universe. It is a melody that originates from heaven. It is a song and proclamation of judgment, which will usher in the coming of the King of angels—the Lord Jesus Christ. It is a song that will feature the very trumpet of the archangel, and it will be sung with a loud and resonant, clarion voice. The whole universe will hear it! This song will usher in the judgments and purifications of Jesus Christ upon the New Earth—a sound that will mark a stark division— between what is true and false; what is good and evil; and what is profane and what is holy.

And there was war in heaven: Michael and his angels fought against the dragon; and the dragon fought and his angels, and prevailed not; neither was their place found any more in heaven.

(Revelation 12:7–8)

The Time of Michael

I believe we are living in what the Bible refers to as the "time of Michael." The time is soon, my friend. And it is urgent for all of us who name the name of Jesus to draw close to Him and to love and obey His commandments. Walking in the fruit of the spirit of love, humility, and meekness are the only sure protection in the coming day of the Lord.

Before the decree bring forth, before the day pass as the chaff, before the fierce anger of the LORD come upon you, before the day of the LORD'S anger come upon you. Seek ye the LORD, all ye meek of the earth, which have wrought his judgment; seek righteousness, seek meekness: it may be ye shall be hid in the day of the LORD'S anger. (Zephaniah 2:2-3)

It is time for we the bride of Christ to close our eyes and to ask the Holy Spirit to reveal to us what a beautiful bride we truly are in Christ. It is time for all of us to pray and to begin to see ourselves as totally complete in Him. It is time to abide in Him. It is time to fulfill the Great Commission and to make disciples of all the nations. Time is running out for you and me to fill up the cup of our reward. The day is far spent and the night is at hand. The song of Michael is about to be sung. For who can stand before the power of God Almighty and His mighty archangels who with flaming swords will descend from on high to defend Israel and to establish the New Jerusalem.

The song of Michael is a song of purity and holiness. It's a song that enforces the full authority of God upon rebellious free wills and false religious spirits which now inhabit the earth and who refuse to joyfully submit to God's commandments. The spirit of Michael will counteract the effeminate, Jezebel spirit of self-exalters and seducers. The spirit of Michael will always counteract the spirit of glamour, celebrity, vanity, and the principality of "Hollywood-style praise," which has now all but taken over worship in the church in the West. God hates the spirit of rebellion, self-important pride, and arrogance. God will purify His altars with fresh holy fire from on high and with the flaming sword of Michael the archangel.

When his trumpet sounds and his voice is raised to proclaim the coming of the King, who will be able to stand in His presence?

Behold, I will send my messenger, and he shall prepare the way before me: and the Lord, whom ye seek, shall suddenly come to his temple, even the messenger of the

130

covenant, whom ye delight in: behold, he shall come, saith the LORD of hosts. But who may abide the day of his coming? and who shall stand when he appeareth? for he is like a refiner's fire, and like fullers' soap: And he shall sit as a refiner and purifier of silver. (Malachi 3:1–3)

Because We Believe

And they that be wise shall shine as the brightness of the firmament; and they that turn many to righteousness as the stars for ever and ever. (Daniel 12:3)

Is not God in the height of heaven? and behold the height of the stars, how high they are. (Job 22:12)

And I John saw the holy city, new Jerusalem, coming down from God out of heaven, prepared as a bride adorned for her husband....and there came unto me one of the seven angels which had the seven vials full of the seven last plagues, and talked with me, saying, Come hither, I will show thee the bride, the Lamb's wife.

(Revelation 21:2, 9)

(Italian)

Guarda fuori e' gia' mattina
Questo e' un giorno che recorderai
Alzati in fetta e vai
C'e chi crede in te
Non ti arrendere

Once in every life

There comes a time
We walk out all alone
And into the light
The moment is soon my friend
We shall see the bride of Him
When we close our eyes

Like stars across the sky
E per avvincere
Tu dovrai vincere
We were born to shine
All of us here because we believe

Guarda avanti e non voltarti mai
Accarezza con I sogni tuoi
Le tue speranze e poi
Verso il giorno che verra'
C'e' un traguardo la'

Like stars across the sky
E per avvincere
Tu dovrai vincere
All of us here because we believe

Non arrenderti
Qualcuno e' con te

Like stars across the sky
We were born to shine

132

E per avvincere
Dovrai vincere
E allora vincerai

Music by David Foster
Italian Lyrics by Andrea Bocelli
English Lyrics by Amy Foster Gillies
Orchestra Arrangement by Bill Ross
© Peer Songs Itality S.r.l./Universal Music
Publishing
Sugar S.r.L./ Almud Edizioni Musicali S.r. l.

All Hail the Truth (Ave Verum)

And it is the Spirit that beareth witness, because the Spirit is truth. (1 John 5:6)

Jesus saith unto him, I am the way, the truth, and the life: no man cometh unto the Father, but by me. (John 14:6)

Latin

Attende domini et Miserere
Hear my prayer and have
compassion on me O God
Quia peccavimus ti bi
Forgive my sins
Attende
Hear me
Et Miserere
Have mercy
Et domini
O God

Ave Verum
"Hail Truth"
Corpus Natum
Everyone sing and worship
Pie Gesu
Precious Jesus
Agnus Dei

Lamb of God

A silent mystery
The break of dawn
An angel flies across eternity

I see the rising son
Perpetual love
And hear the seraph's song
Of truth and love

Chorus (Latin)

Ave Verum
"Hail Truth"
Corpus Natum
Everyone sing and worship
Pie Gesu
Precious Jesus
Agnus Dei
Lamb of God

You are the way the truth,
The life and the Door
There's no one else my God
That I adore
You're the mighty great I am
You're the lion and the lamb
The tribe of Judah
You are

I will surrender to You
All that I am
And I will yield to Your master plan
You're the mighty great I AM
Your truth will always stand
Forever, Lord, my God

The battle ranges on
Good versus evil
The truth is must prevail
All hail the truth
For You are the truth and light
You're the God of power and might
Of all the universe
My God

Ave Verum
Music by Robert Prizeman and Ian Tilley
(MCPS)
(Some Latin lyrics adopted by Freddy Hayler
for Agnus Dei Rizet) © 2004 EMI Records Ltd.

Journey Into Heaven

Some day
One day
One way

(from the song Evacuation—Narnia
soundtrack)
Music by Harry Gregson-Williams © 2005
Disney Records

Celestial Prince

And hath made us kings and priests unto God and his Father; to him be glory and dominion for ever and ever. Amen.

(Revelation 1:6)

But ye are a chosen generation, a royal priesthood, an holy nation, a peculiar people; that ye should shew forth the praises of him who hath called you out of darkness into his marvelous light.

(1 Peter 2:9)

Sono in questo posto
I'm here in this place

D'acgua fresca e cristale
Of fresh crystal waters

Acqua Sorgiva d'amore e luce
A soothing spring of love and light

Fiamma di fuoco
In a fiery blaze

Calma dall'acqua
Now cooled by its waters

Un angelo vestito
An angel's robe of lavender

Io abbracciero
Will I embrace

Chorus

**I am a heavenly man
Cleansed in the waters from celestial lands
I am a priestly bride prepared for the Throne
Destined to serve
Destined to live
Destined to know
A new home in this place
I am a young child here
My old life now an empty shell to leave alone**

Chorus

**I'm a heavenly man
Cleansed in the waters of a celestial lands
I am a priestly bride prepared for the throne
I am like a star in the night brightly burning with the purest light**

I am a prince on the way to his throne

From the song "Wunderkind"
Written by Alanis Morisette
Published by Szeretlek Publishing (BMI)
Adm. By BMG Music Publishing/Wonderland
Music Company, Inc. (BMI)

Innocence Restored

How long until they attain to innocence?
(Hosea 8:5 NKJV)

Forasmuch as before him innocency was found in me; and also before thee, O king, have I done no hurt. (Daniel 6:22)

And said, Verily I say unto you, Except ye turn, and become as little children, ye shall in no wise enter into the kingdom of heaven. (Matthew 18:3 ASV)

From the song "The Wardrobe"
Written by Harry Gregson-Williams and
Lisbeth Scott © From Narnia Score Disney
Records

Stay with Me

Abide in me, and I in you.

(John 15:4 <small>ASV</small>*)*

You're everything I know
Whichever way I go
Forever stay with me

Chorus

Venite angeli
Gracious angels
Cantate domino
Who sing to God
Laudate
Praise and exaltation to God
You see me through whenever I'm
afraid
However far away
Forever comfort me
I'm on your side
Which way you choose
In everything I do
Forever stay with me

Music and Lyrics by Robert Prizeman
© 2004 EMI Record Ltd. (MCPS)

I Can Only Imagine

But as it is written, Eye hath not seen, nor ear heard, neither have entered into the heart of man, the things which God hath prepared for them that love him.

(1 Corinthians 2:9)

I can only imagine
What it will be like
When I walk by your side
I can only imagine
What my eyes will see
When Your face is before me
I can only imagine

Surrounded by Your glory
What will my heart feel
Will I dance for You Jesus
Or in awe of you be still
Will I stand in Your presence
Or to my knees will I fall
Will I sing Hallelujah
Will I be able to speak at all
I can only imagine

I can only imagine
When that day comes
And I find myself
Standing in the Son

I can only imagine
When all I will do
Is forever
Forever worship You
I can only imagine
Yeah

I can only imagine when all I will do
Is forever, forever worship You
I can only imagine

© 1999 Mercy Me

IMAGINE

The Company of Angels

Music written by Harry Gregson-Williams
From Narnia score "Western Woods"
© 2005 Walt Disney Records

Can't Take It In

Let not your heart be troubled; you believe in God, believe also in Me. In My Father's house are many mansions; if it were not so, I would have told you. I go to prepare a place for you. And if I go and prepare a place for you, I will come again and receive you to Myself; that where I am, there you may be also. And where I go you know, and the way you know.

(John 14:1–4 NKJV)

Now to him who is able to do immeasurably more than all we ask or imagine, according to his power that is at work within us, to him be glory in the church and in Christ Jesus throughout all generations, for ever and ever! Amen.

(Ephesians 3:20–21 NIV)

Non posso chindere
I can't close my eyes
Gli occhi
They're wide awake
Tutti capelli nel corpo
Every hair on my body
Ho amore per questo
Loves this place
Devo fare posto per
I've got to make room
quest sentimento
for this lovely feeling
Cosa piu grande di me
Its something much bigger than me

Non puo essere
It couldn't be
Piu bella
Anymore beautiful
It couldn't be anymore lovely
Sei tutto che voglio
You're all I've ever wanted or needed

"Can't take it in"
Written by Imogen Heap.Published by Walt Disney Music Company (ASCAP)/Rondor Music (London) Lrd. (PRS)

Holy, Holy, Holy Lord
God of power, and might
Heaven and earth are full of Your
glory
Hosanna
Hosanna
In the highest
Hosanna in the highest
Holy, holy, holy Lord
God of power and might
Blessed is He who comes in the
name of the Lord.
Hosanna, Hosanna in the highest!

From the Song "Sanctus" by Kirk Dearman
© 1996 Expressions of Praise

A New Heaven

Now I saw a new heaven and a new earth, for the first heaven and the first earth had passed away. Also there was no more sea. Then I, John, saw the holy city, New Jerusalem, coming down out of heaven from God, prepared as a bride adorned for her husband. (Revelation 21:1-2 NKJV)

Do not fear therefore; you are of more value than many sparrows.

(Matthew 10:31 NKJV)

Forasmuch then as the children are partakers of flesh and blood, he also himself likewise took part of the same; that through death he might destroy him that had the power of death, that is, the devil.

(Hebrews 2:14)

Be not afraid
For I am with You
And my love is great
Even greater than
death and the grave

Chorus (Latin)

Illumina, Infinita **(Infinite Light)**
Immanuel Perpetua **(God with us forever)**

And there shall be
No more death
Neither sorrow
Nor crying
For these have all passed away

Ilumina, Infinita **(Infinite Light)**
Immanuel, Perpetua **(God with us forever)**

And then I saw
A new Heaven
And the first earth
And the first earth
Have all passed away

Ilumina, Infinita
Immanuel, Perpetua . . .

Lyrics from Book of Revelation
Music by Robert Prizeman
Additional Lyrics Freddy Hayler
© *2004 EMI Records*

It Is Finished
(Superavi—Victory!)

For the earth shall be filled with the knowledge of the glory of the LORD, as the waters cover the sea. (Habbakuk 2:14)

Will you not revive us again, that your people may rejoice in you?
(Psalm 85:6 NIV)

The day is here
To reach all of the nations in His name
The time is short
Before Christ will return again
Why don't you call on Him
Believe in Him
Go forth to battle
Into the fray
Let us now pray for this new day
Revival for all the U.S.A.
Yeah
It is finished
Jesus has won
America your day has come

The time is now
To turn to Jesus and repent with all of our hearts

Revival now
For all America today
L.A. You'll seek Him
N.Y. Believe in Him
Chicago, Dallas to Frisco Bay
Boston, Carolina will see the day
When all our nation will kneel and say
It is finished
Jesus has won
For by His stripes we've overcome
From Alabama to the gulf of Mexico
Louisiana all the way to Idaho
God's people are praying for revival
Not just in your town but for all land to know
God's Holy Presence to deliver us!
Revive us again
Superavi, Superavi! Latin (It is finished)
Victory!
Now go!
America your last hope is the Lord to revive us again

"Miserere" Written by Zucchero and Bono © 1992 PolyGram Italia Srl/Zucchero and Fornaciari Music Srl

Jesus I Love You

And now these three remain: faith, hope and love. But the greatest of these is love.

(1 Corinthians 13:13 NIV)

For God so loved the world, that he gave his only begotten Son, that whosoever believeth in him should not perish, but have everlasting life. (John 3:16)

That if thou wilt confess with your mouth the Lord Jesus, and shalt believe in thine heart that God hath raised him from the dead, thou shalt be saved.

(Romans 10:9)

Dios, te amo,
Lord, I love You,
Dios, te necesito
Lord, I need You,
Dios, te amo
Lord, I love You,
Te necesito
I need You.
Jesus, te alavo,
Jesus, I praise You,
Jesus, te adoro,
Jesus, I adore You,
Jesus, te alavo y te adoro,

Jesus, I praise You and I adore You,
Tu eres mi Dios,
You are My God,
Mi todo en todo,
My all in all
Cuando oro a Ti
When I pray to You,
Mi corazon sincero es,
Let my heart be true,
Para amarte
To love You
Ahora y para siempre
And to love You forever
Para que seas mi primer amor
To make You my first love, Lord.
Todo mi vida.
For all my life.

Dialogue

My friend, listen to me,
You say, life is too hard,
Why must it be this way?
Yes, life is dark and gloomy
Without Jesus Christ, the light of the world
But today you can ask Him into your life
And have a new heart and say with me...

Jesus, I love You,
Jesus, te amo,
Jesus, I need You,
Jesus, te necesito,
Jesus, I really love You,
Jesus, te amo tanto y
And I need You,
Te necesito,
You are my God
Tu eres mi Dios,
My all in all,
Mi todo en todo,
As I pray to You
Cuando oro a Ti,
Let my heart be true!
Mi corazon sincero es
To love You
Para amarte
And to love You forever!
Ahora y para siempre!
To make You my first love, Lord!
Para que seas mi primer amor!
For all my life
Todo mi vida
To love You, Lord
Te amo, Senor!

Dialogue

Escuchame amigo,
La vida es muy dura,

La vida no tiene sentido
Hasta que conosca a Cristo, tu
Salvador!

Jesus, te amo
Jesus, I love You,
Todo my vida,
For all my life,
Jesus, te amo,
Jesus, I love You,
Jesus, te necesito,
Jesus, I need You,
Jesus, te amo, te necesito.
Jesus, I love You, I need You.
Come on, surrender.
Surrender.
Surrender.
Rendirse
Rendirse
Surrender.
Surrender.
Por todo vida.
Por todo vida.
Por todo vida.
Por todo vida.
Rendirse.

From Mai Piu Cosi Lontano
M. Malavasi. English Lyrics: Freddy Hayler
Cuando oro a Ti, my corazon sincero es...
© 1999, 2001 Insieme S.r.l.
Published in USAby Sugar-Melodi, Inc.

Mattina Stelle
(Morning Star of Heaven)

My voice shalt thou hear in the morning,
O LORD; in the morning will I direct my
prayer unto thee, and will look up.

(Psalm 5:3)

And I will give him the morning star. He
that hath an ear, let him hear what the
Spirit saith unto the churches.

(Revelation 2:28–29)

Verse 1—Italian

Puro le stelle nel cielo
(Pure as the stars of Heaven)
La luna balla nel mare
(As the moonlight dances on the sea)
Una stella notta vedi
(One starry night I saw Your light)
Una luce nel' orizzonte
(Rising upon the horizon)
Luce pura e lucida
(A light so pure and bright)
Brillante con amore
(So brilliant with love)
Luce radiosa che
(A light more radiant than)

La luna e le stelle
(The moon and stars above)
Piu lucida le stelle celeste
(Brighter than the stars of Heaven)
O mattina stella e gloria
(O Morningstar of glory)
Dammi luce per adorarti
(Now shine upon me as I adore You)
Dios da al cuore fuoco
(God fill my heart with Your fire)
Fuoco divino del amore
(The fire of Your divine love)
O Dio, mai ho sognato
(Oh God, I never could have dreamed)
Tuo amore
(Your love)
Mi trovava vivere dentro
(Could find me)
Questa tempesta quando le cose
(Living in such stormy weather)
Vivente non vanno bene
(And when things in life don't go my way)
Perche c'ho a te!
(It's okay as long as I'm with You)

Verse 2

Bright are the stars that shine above
As moonlight dances on the waters
My love for You grows every day
My love for You will last forever
Through heartache and the years
The laughter and the tears
Your beauty it has grown
And your faithfulness has shown
You are my One true God and Savior

Chorus 2—Spanish

O, Jesús, te amo tanto
(Oh Jesus, how I love You)
Mi soledad no esta mas en mi vida
(All loneliness is vanished from my life)
Tu amor es como la luna,
(Your love is like the moonlight)
Reflejando el amor en mi alma
(Reflecting Your sunlight to my soul)

Oh, I never could have dreamed
My life in You Lord
Could bring so much love forever
And when things in life
Don't go my way
When times get tough
Well that's okay
I've put my trust in You
I never could have dreamed
My life with You Lord
Could bring so much love forever
And when things in life
Don't go my way
When times get tough
Well that's okay
God's strength will see
Me through
It's all okay
I put my trust in You

Written by D. Farina A. Maggio
English Lyrics by Freddy Hayler
© 1994 Ed. Suvini Zerboni/
Sugar Melodi U.S.A. 2001

The Song of Michael

Not everyone who says to me, "Lord, Lord" will enter the kingdom of Heaven, but only he who does the will of my Father who is in heaven. Many will say to Me in that day, "Lord, Lord"....Then I will tell them plainly, "I never knew you. Away from me, you evildoers!"

(Matthew 7:21–23 NIV)

How often would I have gathered thy children together, even as a hen gathereth her chickens under her wings, and ye would not! (Matthew 23:37)

I know thy works, that thou art neither cold nor hot: I would thou wert cold or hot. So then because thou art lukewarm, and neither cold nor hot, I will spue thee out of my mouth. (Revelation 3:15–16)

Jesus wept. (John 11:35)

Verse 1

Angels of HIS Presence
Let there be no singing
For it's a time to weep now
For His precious Bride

Do they love Him?
Or do they use Him?
The time is short before He comes

Chorus 1

This hymn is what I'm singing
Lament of tears and weeping
Hear, My heart oh Bride so blessed
Is there longing in your heart?
All He wants is to embrace you
Hold you in His arms and love you
He's Your Creator God
When will you come to HIM?
Interlude (so says the Lord...)

Verse 2

There are those who say that
They really know Me
But the day will come when
I must tell them this
You never knew Me
You never loved Me
With all Your heart and all your
soul

Chorus 2

Can you hear the angels weeping?

Praying that the Bride will hear Me
And leave this world and all her
idols
Jezebel and all her lust
And sin

Interlude

Lucifer will not prevail
Oh My Bride how I adore You
Come return unto Your first love
I will cleanse You in My Blood
For I'm coming for You soon
I will come and gather you

Coming for My faithful few

(These lyrics were inspired by an 18th-century sermon by Charles Finney entitled "True Saints.")

Then Jesus sent the multitude away, and went into the house: and his disciples came unto him, saying, Declare unto us the parable of the tares of the field.

(Matthew 13:36)

He that soweth the good seed is the Son of man; the field is the world; the good seed are the children of the kingdom; but the tares are the children of the wicked one; the enemy that sowed them is the devil; the harvest is the end of the world; and the reapers are the angels. As therefore the tares are gathered and burned in the fire; so shall it be in the end of this world. The Son of man shall send forth his angels, and they shall gather out of his kingdom all things that offend, and them which do iniquity.

(Matthew 13:37–41)

And before him shall be gathered all nations: and he shall separate them one from another, as a shepherd divideth his sheep from the goats: and he shall set the sheep on his right hand, but the goats on the left. (Matthew 25:32–33)

Michael (in Hebrew, "who is like God?"): a general among the celestial archangels, a heavenly prince, and a patron angel of Israel, he champions God's people over the fallen archangel Lucifer (Daniel 12:1). He is a heavenly prince who stands up and intercedes for the saints of God. (See Daniel 10:13, 20.) In the final battle he will lead the celestial hosts of heaven to battle against and destroy the forces of Lucifer and hell (Revelation 12:7).

In almost all ancient Jewish literature, Michael is the vindicator of Israel against Edom, Sodom, and all the wicked forces of hell. He is also the head administrator of the heavenly records, the chief librarian who is in charge of recording all the thoughts, words, and actions of every soul sent into the world by God Almighty (Acts 7:38). He was an intermediary between God and Moses. In Jude 9, he disputed over the body of Moses with Satan.

Credits

Producer: *Freddy Hayler*
Soundtrack and Musical Arrangement:
John DeVries, Steve Errante, Freddy Hayler
Package Design and Layout: *Ford Design*
Photography: *Brownie Harris Photography,
New York, NY and Wilmington, NC, Marshall
Marvelli*
Transcription Production: *Freddy Hayler,
Steve Errante, Larry Hall and John DeVries*
Conceptual Design, Writing, and Editing:
Freddy and Anne Hayler
Publishing: *Golden Altar Publishing
Song of Angels Publishing*
Chief Audio Engineer and Mix:
Dan Oxley/D&D Productions, Nashville TN.
**Sound Engineers and Computer
Programming:** *J. K. Loftin, Wilmington, N.C.*
Additional Recording Studios:
*David's Song Production, Nashville, TN
Mastering: Benny Quinn, Masterphonics,
Nashville, TN*
Clothiers: *Neal Fleishman, Dennis Sugar and
The Woody Wilson Collection*
MusiciansContractor: *David's Song
Production/Nashville String Machine*
Strings: *David Davidson/ Concert Master*
Violin: *Alan Umstead, David Angell,
Janet Askey, Karen Winklemann, Zebena
Bowers, Bruce Christensen, Catherine
Umstead, Pamela Suxfin*
Viola: *Idalynn Besser, Monisa Angell*
Cello: *Bob Mason, Lynn Peithman,
Bradley Mansell*
Piano: *Rolin Mains*

Lead guitar: *Paul Brannon*
Piccolo Tumpet Solo: *Dan Oxley*
Trumpet: *Jeff Bailey*
Oboe and English horn: *Bobby Taylor,
Roger Weismeyer*
Clarinet: *Matthew Davich*
Harp: *Mary Hoepfinger*
Percussion: *Mike Mann*
Flute, Alto Flute, Piccolo:
Brendon McKinney
French Horn: *Beth Beeson, Jennifer Kummer,
Calvin Smith, Steve Patrick*
Conductor: *John DeVries, Blaire Masters*

*Mailing Address:
Golden Altar Records
P. O. Box 10740
Wilmington, NC 28404 U. S. A.
Tel: 910-262-4137   Fax: 910-270-3240*

**Personal Management and International
Representation:**
*Declare His Glory Ministries International
Kingdom Management (904) 646-2626
2222 Walkers Glenn Lane
Jacksonville, FL 32246
Golden Altar Records (910) 270-3240 (Fax)*

*Email: Jesusisglorious@cs.com
Email: kingdommanagement@hotmail.com
Official Website: www.songofangels.com
Additional music available at www.
FreddyHaylerTenor.com*

PART III

AN URGENT INVITATION

God's Plan of Salvation

You may ask yourself at this point what must I do to go to heaven when I die? The Lord wants you to know that you can be assured of your salvation and that you can go to heaven.

These things have I written unto you that believe on the name of the Son of God; that ye may know that ye have eternal life, and that ye may believe on the name of the Son of God. (1 John 5:13)

What must you do then? First, you must acknowledge that you are a sinner and repent of your sins. That means you must turn from the way you have been living and turn to a new and living way, which is following the life of Jesus Christ. The Bible says, "*All have sinned and fall short of the glory of God*" (Romans 3:23 NKJV). Through sin, the gate to the garden in paradise was closed to mankind. But through Christ, the gate has now been opened for all who would repent and who would accept Christ as Lord and Savior. No matter how good you think

you are, you can never get into heaven on your own merit. You must repent and turn from your sins to where God can help you—God's grace is sufficient.

For by grace are ye saved through faith; and that not of yourselves: it is the gift of God. (Ephesians 2:8)

Second, you must trust Jesus Christ for your salvation. Jesus died for you and took your sins upon Him when He died on the cross. He shed His blood for you. And He now offers forgiveness and salvation as a free gift to you.

For the wages of sin is death; but the gift of God is eternal life through Jesus Christ our Lord. (Romans 6:23)

Please do not procrastinate any longer, for God is calling you to His eternal salvation at this very moment.

Wherefore as the Holy Ghost saith, To day if ye will hear his voice, harden not your hearts, as in the provocation, in the day of temptation in the wilderness. (Hebrews 3:7–8)

Behold, now is the accepted time; behold, now is the day of salvation.

(2 Corinthians 6:2)

Scriptures and Prayer for Salvation

May we all yield to His Friendship and His Lordship while there is yet time to do so. His grace is more than sufficient to rescue any who will call upon Him. Just call upon His name with your whole heart and you will feel His saving presence surround you! Just say:

"Lord Jesus, I confess with my mouth that You are my Lord and God. I repent of all my sins and ask You to forgive me and cleanse me by the blood of Jesus shed at the cross of Calvary. Come into my heart, Jesus, and make me born again by Your Spirit. Fill me with Your Holy Spirit and empower me by Your grace to submit to Your Lordship. I totally surrender to Your will, Lord Jesus, and for the rest of my life I am totally Yours."

God knows the feeble human frame. He knows how blind and ignorant we can be. Thankfully, He has not made salvation some mystical, esoteric difficult formula to understand. Unlike other religions, salvation is offered freely from heaven and can be easily accepted by anyone without respect of persons. God has made salvation very simple—simple but profound. He's made it so simple that all a person needs to do is confess with their mouth and sincerely believe in their heart that Jesus Christ is Lord.

That if thou shalt confess with thy mouth the Lord Jesus, and shalt believe in thine heart that God hath raised him from the dead, thou shalt be saved. For with the heart man believeth unto righteousness; and with the mouth confession is made unto salvation. (Romans 10:9–10)

God wants all of us to be *assured*; He wants all of us to know for certain we are saved and that it is a difficult thing for a truly saved person to habitually and continually desire to sin against God.

These things have I written unto you that believe on the name of the Son of God;

that ye may know that ye have eternal life, and that ye may believe on the name of the Son of God. (1 John 5:13)

A newly constituted butterfly must eat sweet nectar and will not return to "chomping" on a leaf.

Therefore if any man be in Christ, he is a new creature: old things are passed away; behold, all things are become new.
(2 Corinthians 5:17)

To those who are proud and conceited, to those who are in the world and consider themselves "learned," all of this might sound too simple and straightforward. To this, the apostle Paul said,

For the preaching of the cross is to them that perish foolishness; but unto us which are saved it is the power of God.
(1 Corinthians 1:18)

Jesus the King is coming. He will come! Heaven is a real place. Heaven has a real location. Heaven has a real King and Judge. If there is no heaven, then there will be no King of heaven. In John chap-

ter six, Jesus said He was the Bread of life that came down from heaven. If there is no heaven, then there is no spiritual food and sustenance. If there is no heaven, there is no forgiveness, no salvation, and no resurrection. Heaven is a very important doctrine you see. The Bible tells us to look up, for our redemption draws near.

Dear friend, your only ticket, your only passport to the heavenly city of God is Jesus!

Jesus saith unto him, I am the way, the truth, and the life: no man cometh unto the Father, but by me. (John 14:6)

Neither is there salvation in any other: for there is none other name under Heaven given among men, whereby we must be saved. (Acts 4:12)

If you will accept Him as Lord and Savior, you will walk through the garden of paradise with Jesus and His angels. You will see your Christian loved ones once again. You will see those precious personalities you loved so much while they lived on earth. You may not see them again on this side of glory but you will see them again in the Celestial City! You need to start looking to heaven and be aware that time is short. You need to look up, for your redemption draws nigh. Are you ready to see Jesus? Do you walk in heavenly peace, joy, and holiness? Are you living holy in this life so that you will be ready to live holy in glory?

Life is so short. People are here today and then are gone tomorrow. So many pay too much attention to things that are not important. When compared to eternity, the life you are now living is so very short. One day you are young, and the next day you are old. One day you have all the strength and energy you need and in a few years it's gone.

I am he that liveth, and was dead; and, behold, I am alive for evermore, Amen; and have the keys of hell and of death.
(Revelation 1:18)

God loves you without measure and has sent His "best" to so that you could be saved.

For God so loved the world, that he gave his only begotten Son, that whosoever believeth in him should not perish, but have everlasting life. (John 3:16)

And His goal is not only to save you but to conform you into His image. He desires for you to become part of the royal family—sons and daughters of the living God!

But as many as received him, to them gave he power to become the sons of God, even to them that believe on his name.
(John 1:12)

The question remains, are you open to hearing His voice?

Behold, I stand at the door, and knock: if any man hear my voice, and open the door, I will come in to him, and will sup with him, and he with me.
(Revelation 3:20)

It doesn't matter what sins you've committed or what race or ethnic background you are from—God will save you for He is no respecter of persons.

For whosoever shall call upon the name of the Lord shall be saved.

(Romans 10:13, emphasis added)

Therefore being justified by faith, we have peace with God through our Lord Jesus Christ. (Romans 5:1)

God has done everything necessary to make your salvation possible. The choice is yours. You must personally receive Christ and make a solid decision to follow Him. You must believe that He died on the cross and rose again from the dead so that you can have eternal life. Therefore, right now, I ask you to pray a prayer asking Christ to forgive you and to invite Him into your heart as your Lord and Savior.

I would like to offer you another prayer of salvation that you can repeat to Jesus.

Say this prayer and repeat it out loud with sincerity until you have that assurance in your heart.

Dear Jesus, I am a sinner. I repent of my sins. I am sorry that I ever sinned against You. Forgive my sins right now. Cleanse me by Your blood, Lord Jesus. Make me clean. Remove evil from my heart. I ask You to come into my heart. Come into my heart, Lord Jesus. I receive You as my Lord and Savior. I believe that You came to this earth and died on the cross for me. I believe you are the Son of the Living God. Amen.

If you have prayed this prayer with me and sincerely believed what you prayed, you can be assured that you are saved. The apostle Paul had such confidence when he wrote:

For the which cause I also suffer these things: nevertheless I am not ashamed: for I know whom I have believed, and am persuaded that he is able to keep that which I have committed unto him against that day. (2 Timothy 1:12)

If you have asked Jesus into your heart and totally committed your life to Him, God has forgiven you and you have been adopted into your royal family. He also promises to save you and to bring you into His heavenly kingdom forever. He wants you to feel secure in this.

> *And this is the record, that God hath given to us eternal life, and this life is in his Son. He that hath the Son hath life; and he that hath not the Son of God hath not life. These things have I written unto you that believe on the name of the Son of God; that ye may know that ye have eternal life, and that ye may believe on the name of the Son of God.*
>
> (1 John 5:11-13)

God cannot lie. What He has promised will come to pass. For you who have trusted Christ for salvation, heaven is your destination. Heaven will be your home.

How to Be Baptized in the Holy Spirit

No Christian ministry should ever preach or teach the gospel without giving an invitation for folks to get born again and filled with the Holy Spirit. Because so many evangelical and Charismatic leaders have taken these things for granted, the church has had little real growth since 1988 in America. We need

more than just an invitation that says, "You can give your heart to Christ right now." We need to give the people the full gospel—that they need to repent from sin and become born again so that they can be filled with the Holy Spirit and go on to live unto righteousness.

The Holy Spirit and Fire

> *I indeed baptize you with water unto repentance: but he that cometh after me is mightier than I, whose shoes I am not worthy to bear: he shall baptize you with the Holy Ghost, and with fire.*
>
> (Mathew 3:11)

The next step is to ask Jesus to fill you with the Person of the Holy Spirit in the *baptism of the Holy Spirit*. Without the baptism of the Holy Spirit, it will be difficult to persevere through all the moral chaos in this hour. The demonic forces of hell have unleashed their full fury upon every soul who calls on the name of Christ. The devil's time is short and he desires for *his* family to be enlarged and to spend eternity with him and his abode of unmitigated wickedness and destruction. In this hour of darkness, simply having an intellectual grasp of what Christ has promised through the Holy Spirit is not enough. We need to be filled with the Holy Spirit. We cannot save ourselves but must fully depend on the enabling power of the Holy Spirit who works within us to save us from our sins—*for He is not a God who saves us in our sins.*

We are to repent from sin and yield our lives to the Holy Spirit who works the grace of God within our hearts both to do and to will His good pleasure. (See Philippians 2:13.) Because of the supernatural pull of the demonic forces of pride, lust and evil in this hour, the righteous remnant will need to avail themselves of all the supernatural power that God offers through the Baptism of the Holy Spirit. If one hundred years ago, Dwight L. Moody found it necessary to ask for this experience, so should we. He testified that the fruit of his evangelistic ministry doubled after getting alone with God and asking Christ to baptize him in the Holy Spirit.

If Charles Finney said that he lied prostrate in the woods for three days pleading to God for this experience—that's good enough for me! We all should do whatever it takes to seek God and to ask God for this mighty blessing from on high! Ask the Lord Jesus right now to fill you with the baptism of the Holy Spirit and fire! Delay no longer!

The Lord Jesus understands man's natural fear concerning the unknown. But the Holy Spirit is a gentleman and will only immerse a believer who willingly desires to be filled by Him.

Consider These Following Texts

If ye then, being evil, know how to give good gifts unto your children: how much more shall your heavenly Father give the Holy Spirit to them that ask him?
(Luke 11:13)

Some teach that this was only a *dispensational* event necessary to birth the new church. The Bible does not say that. As a matter of fact, Jesus said that a new believer will be more effective in witnessing the gospel after being empowered with the dynamite power of the Holy Spirit filling their entire being.

> And, being assembled together with them, commanded them that they should not depart from Jerusalem, but wait for the promise of the Father, which, saith he, ye have heard of me. For John truly baptized with water; but ye shall be baptized with the Holy Ghost not many days hence.
> (Acts 1:4-5)

> And when the day of Pentecost was fully come, they were all with one accord in one place. And suddenly there came a sound from heaven as of a rushing mighty wind, and it filled all the house where they were sitting. And there appeared unto them cloven tongues like as of fire, and it sat upon each of them. And they were all filled with the Holy Ghost, and began to speak with other tongues, as the Spirit gave them utterance.
> (Acts 2:1-4)

As you can see from the Scriptures below, this "Pentecostal" experience (or what John Wesley referred to as "a second work of grace") did not cease after the 120 received the baptism of the Holy Spirit in the upper room.

> He said unto them, Have ye received the Holy Ghost since ye believed? And they said unto him, We have not so much as heard whether there be any Holy Ghost.... Then said Paul, John verily baptized with the baptism of repentance, saying unto the people, that they should believe on him which should come after him, that is, on Christ Jesus. When they heard this, they were baptized in the name of the Lord Jesus. And when Paul had laid his hands upon them, the Holy Ghost came on them; and they spake with tongues, and prophesied.
> (Acts 19:2, 4-6)

Fire on You, Again!

Remember, if you want to be a real effective soul winner, you need the baptism of the Holy Spirit!

> But ye shall receive power, after that the Holy Ghost is come upon you: and ye shall

be witnesses unto me both in Jerusalem, and in all Judea, and in Samaria, and unto the uttermost part of the earth.

(Acts 1:8)

As with the early church, as Spirit-filled believers today, we need to constantly remind ourselves to instruct those who are newly born again regarding this wonderful experience promised by God.

Now when the apostles which were at Jerusalem heard that Samaria had received the word of God, thy sent unto them Peter and John: who, when they were come down, prayed for them, that they might receive the Holy Ghost: (For as yet he was fallen upon non of them: only they were baptized in the name of the Lord Jesus.) Then laid they their hands on them, and they received the Holy Ghost.

(Acts 8:14-17)

When a person is filled with the Holy Spirit this will often be accompanied with supernatural, spiritual gifts such as found in 1 Corinthians 12 through 14.

While Peter yet spoke these words, the Holy Ghost fell on all them, which head the word. And they of the circumcision, which believed, were astonished, as many as came with Peter, because that on the Gentiles also was poured out the gift of the Holy Ghost. For they heard them speak with tongues, and magnify God. Then answered Peter, can any man forbid water, that these should not be baptized, which have received the Holy Ghost as well as we? (Acts 10:44-47)

The greatest fruit of the Holy Spirit is the Christlikeness He will work within the new believer. Also, the Holy Spirit will always magnify God and Jesus Christ and will not draw attention to self or any gifting.

But when the Comforter is come, whom I will send unto you from the Father, even the Spirit of truth, which proceedeth from the Father, he shall testify of me.

(John 15:26)

Of course, the greatest fruit of being totally yielded to the Holy Spirit is evident by the unconditional love of God that pours forth from the heart. As a matter of fact, the spiritual gifts pale in comparison to the ultimate fruit of the Holy Spirit, which is the love of God.

> *Though I speak with the tongues of men and of angels, and have not charity, I am become as sounding brass, or a tinkling cymbal. And though I have the gift of prophecy, and understand all mysteries, and all knowledge; and though I have all faith, so that I could remove mountains, and have not charity, I am nothing.*
>
> (1 Corinthians 13:1–2)

> *But the fruit of the Spirit is love, joy, peace, longsuffering, gentleness, goodness, faith.* (Galatians 5:22)

As important as the fruit is, God in no way negates the gifts of the Holy Spirit as a manifestation of being baptized in the Holy Spirit.

Isaiah, the prophet, wrote centuries earlier of a generation of believers who would yield their tongues to the Holy Spirit:

> *For with stammering lips and another tongue will he speak to this people.*
>
> (Isaiah 28:11)

We find that Isaiah's prophecy was fulfilled upon the day of Pentecost and is testified by the apostle Paul.

> *In the law it is written, With men of other tongues and other lips will I speak unto this people; and yet for all that will they not hear me, saith the Lord.*
>
> (1 Corinthians 14:21)

> *Likewise, the Spirit also helpeth our infirmity: for we know not what we should pray for as we ought; but the Spirit itself maketh intercession for us with groanings which cannot be uttered.*
>
> (Romans 8:26)

The prophet Isaiah and the apostle Paul were not referring to "learned" human languages in these texts. Just because the language that the Holy Spirit gives is unintelligible to the human mind does not disqualify it as a bona-fide gift of God. When Paul spoke about preferring prophecy (that is, speaking the Word of the Lord in a known human language) instead of speaking in tongues in the public meeting-place, he is only referring to the *public use* of tongues and not the *private use* of tongues for personal edification and spiritual warfare. Like the apostle Paul, Jude the brother of James and the half brother of Jesus did not diminish the need for praying in the Spirit.

> But ye, beloved, building up yourselves on your most holy faith, praying in the Holy Ghost. (Jude 1:20)

Paul even boasted to the Corinthians (who were carnal and took pride in their hyper-spirituality and the spiritual gifts they possessed), that he spoke in tongues (his private prayer language) more than any of them.

> For he that speaketh in an unknown tongue speaketh not unto men, but unto God: for no man understandeth him; howbeit in the spirit he speaketh mysteries... for if I pray in an unknown tongue, my spirit prayeth, but my understanding is unfruitful....I thank my God, I speak with tongues more than ye all.
> (1 Corinthians 14:2, 14, 18)

Baptism of Fire

I am not ashamed to inform all of you that there is another baptism that many Christians still need to experience. Yes, at salvation, you "get/obtain" the Father, the Son, and the Holy Spirit. (See Matthew 28:19.) In fact, all Three dwell in you by God's grace, through simple, sincere faith in Jesus Christ! You cannot divide the Trinity. Let me give you an illustration. When you have a guest visit you at your home and you are not there to greet him, you may call out from the kitchen or from another room, "Come on in, I'll be with you in a minute." As the person stands in the foyer, they are in fact waiting to be received. The person is in the house but because that person has manners, they will not just walk in and make themselves at home. You must first leave the kitchen and go and receive your guest in order for him to make himself at home. So it is with the person of the Holy Spirit. At salvation, he is like a guest coming into our home (our temple, which is our spirit, soul, and body). We must then

fully receive Him in order to make our entire home (see 1 Thessalonians 5:23) entirely His!

As believers, we should now want to receive the Holy Spirit and ask Him to fill and inhabit our whole house. This is what John the Baptist spoke of when he said,

> I indeed baptize you with water unto repentance: but he that cometh after me is mightier than I, whose shoes I am not worthy to bear: he shall baptize you with the Holy Ghost and with fire.
>
> (Matthew 3:11)

Jesus also said,

> If ye then, being evil, know how to give good gifts unto your children; how much more shall your heavenly Father give the Holy Spirit to them that ask Him?
>
> (Luke 11:13)

Again, Jesus is a gentleman and will not force any believer to be filled with His Holy Spirit. No believer will ever receive the baptism of the Holy Spirit or any of the gifts of the Spirit without stepping out by faith and seeking them with all their heart. The Spirit's infilling is a gift from God and must be asked for and sought after by a believer.

The baptism of the Holy Spirit involves Jesus as the Baptizer and the medium is the fiery Holy Spirit of God! I ask, therefore, how can one be baptized in fire if he does not know Jesus to begin with? How can you ask someone to do something that you do not know? Some may say, "But I received the Holy Spirit at salvation." In a sense, this is true. You do have the Holy Spirit. But *receiving the baptism of the Holy Spirit* is a different experience altogether. The baptism of the Holy Spirit can occur immediately after one's conversion when one knows to ask for both. (See Acts 2:38.)

We also find that the baptism in the Holy Spirit can also precede water baptism (water baptism is an important part of our obedience and sanctification, but is not a prerequisite for salvation). (See Acts 10:47–48.) But many Christians have not because they ask not or they have not because they do not know to ask. The Holy Spirit is a gentleman. He has manners. He will never force Himself upon anyone without their willingly asking Him to. There must be thirst. There must be hunger. All of us, as believers, should ask Jesus to completely fill us with the Holy Spirit! This empowers one for service. This is what the disciples waited for in the upper room. (See Acts 1:8, 2:1-10.) We need God's "baptisms" in order to avail ourselves of the full measure of the fruit of the Spirit (Galatians 5:22-23), and the supernatural gifts of the Spirit. The apostle Paul taught that we should seek "continual infillings" of the Holy Spirit. One of the ways to stay filled with the Holy Spirit is found in the following passage:

And be not drunk with wine, in which is excess, but be filled [in Greek, meaning "continually"] *with the Spirit, speaking to yourselves in psalms and hymns and spiritual songs, singing and making melody in your heart to the Lord.*
(Ephesians 5:18-19)

Many Christians today are living compromised, worldly, lukewarm, defeated lives because their spiritual "gas tanks" are "half-empty!" They have the water and they have the blood—but they need more of the indwelling of the Holy Spirit!

Who is he that overcometh the world, but he that believeth that Jesus is the Son of God? This is he that came by water and blood, even Jesus Christ; not by water only, but by water and blood. And it is the Spirit that beareth witness, because the Spirit is truth. For there are three that bear record in heaven, the Father, the Word, and the Holy Ghost: and these three are one.
(1 John 5:5-8)

In other words, the entire Trinity is involved with our salvation (this is a mystery—you cannot separate the Godhead!).

You receive the Holy Spirit at salvation. He comes into your heart. But now you need to ask the Lord to take you to the next level. You need to ask for the baptism of the Holy Spirit to fall upon you and to fill you in order to have increased effectiveness in Christian ministry. Otherwise, you are not operating on all cylinders! The 120 of the inner circle of Jesus were hungry enough to pray and seek God's face for ten straight days before the Holy Spirit came upon them mightily in the upper room. (See Acts 2:1–4.) Therefore, ask the Lord Jesus whom you now know and love through your salvation experience to baptize you in the fire of His Holy Spirit as D. L. Moody, R. A. Torrey, Andrew Murray, John Wesley, and Watchman Nee have all done.

New Testament/Spirit-filled Christian Living!

If you want to become an intellectualized Pharisee, don't ask to be filled with the Holy Spirit. If you want to grieve the Holy Spirit, go ahead and continue to live in a state of unbelief, worldliness, and outright sin. If you don't want to walk in power in this hour, go ahead and keep trying to figure everything out in your head without yielding your heart and trusting the Holy Spirit totally.

If you want to flow in the supernatural and walk in victory and holiness during this evil hour, you need the baptism in the Holy Spirit! Having this wonderful experience will lead to your operating more and more in the gifts of the Holy Spirit and will cause you to continually walk in the Holy Spirit's infillings. Your entire ministry will have increased spiritual fruit beyond what you can imagine possible! (See Ephesians 3:20–21.)

Decently and In Order

It is intriguing to study the apostle Paul's explanation to the church of Corinth (they were misusing the gifts) regarding the spiritual gifts God has promised to all His people who desire them. (1 Corinthians 14:1.) Paul commanded all of us, regardless of our denominational backgrounds, to earnestly desire the spiritual gifts of the Holy Spirit. Some of these gifts are revelatory, some are power gifts, etc., but whether the greatest or the least, why would any Christian not desire all of them?

Regarding the gift of tongues Paul said,

He that speaketh in an unknown tongue edifieth himself. (1 Corinthians 14:4)

For if I pray in an unknown tongue, my spirit prayeth, but my understanding is unfruitful. (1 Corinthians 14:14)

Regarding the other supernatural gifts, Paul said,

To another faith by the same Spirit; to another the gifts of healing by the same Spirit; to another the working of miracles; to another prophecy; to another discerning of spirits; to another divers kinds of tongues; to another the interpretation of tongues: but all these worketh that one and the self same Spirit, dividing to every man severally as he will.
(1 Corinthians 12:9–10)

Praying in the Spirit

When Paul spoke of someone needing to interpret tongues, he was referring to the *public use* of tongues in the assembly, not the private use of tongues. Regarding the spiritual gifts more than anything else, Christians tend to confuse this the most. Praying in the Spirit will edify you spiritually and will make you more cognizant of the realities and activities of God's glory realm. You and I, as well, should not be bound by our circumstances and should be able to contact God through prayer in the Spirit in the heavenly realm. (See Jude 1:20.)

I thank my God I speak with tongues more than you all.
(1 Corinthians 14:18 NKJV)

Here, Paul referred to his private prayer life, not the public use of tongues that he was correcting in the church at Corinth. All of 1 Corinthians 14 is an attempt to set these revelatory gifts in divine order. The apostle Paul never diminished the private prayer language at all but rather said,

For he that speaketh in an unknown tongue speaketh not unto men, but unto God: for no man understandeth him;

howbeit in the spirit he speaketh myster-
ies. But he that prophesieth speaketh unto
men to edification, and exhortation, and
comfort. He that speaketh in an unknown
tongue edifieth himself; but he that proph-
esieth edifieth the church.

(1 Corinthians 14:2–4)

Paul's habit of praying in tongues and in the Holy Spirit constantly was probably at least one of the major reasons why he was so sensitive to the things of God and had so many supernatural encounters with God and His angels. It's disappointing that so many evangelical teachers preach without distinguishing, as Paul did, between the private and public uses of praying or speaking in the language of the Holy Spirit!

Love Jesus

And now, my friend, love Jesus with all of your heart, your soul, your mind, and your strength, and love your neighbor and your enemies even as you love yourself. For the final, end-time revival will be a revival of love that even the world

cannot deny! Forgive all. Keep a short account and perform restitution and restoration where it is needful. Prepare your hearts. The shout of the Bridegroom is nearer than you think and the angels of the Lord are always standing nearby to help you in time of need.

All of our love in Christ! Jesus loves you and adores you!

–Freddy Hayler